THE CENTER FOR A STATELESS SOCIETY
MUTUAL EXCHANGE

FREE MARKETS & CAPITALISM?

DO FREE MARKETS ALWAYS PRODUCE A CORPORATE ECONOMY?

ORGANIZED BY
CORY MASSIMINO
Mutual Exchange Coordinator C4SS

EDITED BY
JAMES TUTTLE
Coordinating Director C4SS

COVER ART BY
JEFF WOLFE
Advisor C4SS

"Intellectual property," and the states that enforce it, are the enemies of knowledge, progress, and human life itself. It's time to destroy them.

— Kevin Carson

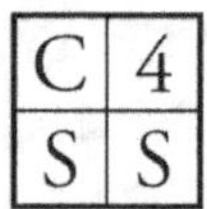

Free Markets & Capitalism?
The Center for a Stateless Society
Mutual Exchange

~~~

Published by CreateSpace
Anno MMXVI

~~~

Interior Book Design & Typesetting
by
Alfred DeStefano III

~~~

The image depicted on the cover of this book is Wenceslaus Hollar's *The Fly and the Ant* (mid-seventeenth century). It is a graphical rendering of Æsop's fable of the same name. The astute reader is encouraged to study this fable in context with the material herewith presented. (See postscript at the end of the present text.)
~~~

We can no longer blind ourselves to the fact that concentrated economic power has become as reckless and ruthless and coercive as concentrated political power.

We can no longer attack subsidies for the poor while supporting even greater subsidies for the rich. We can no longer speak of protecting freedom in the world by turning the world into protective hamlets. We can no longer oppose tyranny by emulating it.

We cannot speak of individual freedom and free communities, self-reliance and self-responsibility, while honoring the assembly line, promoting urban demolition, and making fetish of commodities. We cannot speak of honest work while honest working people are alienated from the work and treated as mere extensions of their machines.

We cannot attack the abuses of arrogant and bureaucratic labor leaders without attacking the abuses of arrogant and bureaucratic industrial and business leaders.

We cannot speak of a land of liberty and a national-security state in the same breath — we must defend freedom at home if we are ever to have freedom in the world.

We cannot speak of a sweet land of liberty when the very land is soured by greed of those who turn the landscape into real estate, who turn the rivers into open sewers, who see in every living thing nothing but a dollar in the process.

—Karl Hess

Our goal is not to assume leadership of existing institutions, but rather to render them irrelevant. We don't want to take over the state or change its policies. We want to render its laws unenforceable. We don't want to take over corporations and make them more "socially responsible." We want to build a counter-economy of open-source information, neighborhood garage manufacturing, Permaculture, encrypted currency and mutual banks, leaving the corporations to die on the vine along with the state.

We do not hope to reform the existing order. We intend to serve as its grave-diggers.

—Kevin Carson

CONTENTS

II. “Free Markets & Capitalism?” C4SS’s October 2015 Mutual Exchange

For M. George van der Meer,
thank you for helping light the way.

"Because of its defining flexibility, anarchism is the thing to rise and meet what's next."

THE C4SS MUTUAL EXCHANGE

I'm happy to announce the official launch of the Center for a Stateless Society's (C4SS) Monthly Mutual Exchange Symposium. C4SS's effort to achieve mutual understanding through exchange is now a monthly project. Mutual Exchange will explore many issues from a variety of different perspectives.

Mutual Exchange is C4SS's goal in two senses: We favor a society rooted in peaceful, voluntary cooperation, and we seek to foster understanding through ongoing dialogue. Mutual Exchange will provide opportunities for conversation about issues that matter to C4SS's audience.

A lead essay, deliberately provocative, will be followed by responses from inside and outside C4SS, a rejoinder by our lead essayist, and further contributions if need be. C4SS is extremely interested in feedback from our readers. Suggestions and comments are enthusiastically encouraged. If you're interested in proposing topics and/or authors for our program to pursue, or if you're interested in participating yourself, please email C4SS's Mutual Exchange Coordinator, Cory Massimino, at cory.massimino@c4ss.org.

I look forward to Mutual Exchange, and to seeing our authors and readers gain a better, fuller understanding through shared dialogue.

DO FREE MARKETS ALWAYS PRODUCE A CORPORATE ECONOMY?

CORY MASSIMINO

What would a free market look like? Most people agree that totally freed markets are nowhere to be seen in today's world. States intruding on voluntary exchange and standing in the way of free association is commonplace across the globe. There are some markets, yes. But they are all, to certain degrees, hampered and regulated, or worse, outlawed. To a certain extent, they are *un-free*. So what do we make of the libertarian notion of completely and absolutely free markets? What do we have in mind when we talk about a "free market"? Is it more or less a vision of modern American capitalism and a corporate dominated economy or is it something radically different? Are there reasons to think a libertarian free market would look a certain way?

The *Monthly Mutual Exchange Symposium* is C4SS's effort to achieve mutual understanding through exchange. October's Mutual Exchange Symposium will explore the dynamics of a market economy characterized by individual, decentralized ownership, contract and voluntary exchange, free competition, entrepreneurial discovery, and spontaneous order. It will seek to discover whether these kinds of institutional arrangements are likely to manifest in traditionally corporate modes of production characterized by a relatively small number of people who control the means of production and investable wealth.

The Center for a Stateless Society will be publishing an essay on the above subject matter every other day starting on October 1st from a diverse range of thinkers. Kevin Carson, C4SS Senior Fellow and Karl Hess Chair in Social Theory, offers his mutualist perspective on this month's issue, arguing, as he has done so many times before, that a freed market, without the "artificial property rights, artificial scarcities, subsidies and monopolistic entry barriers or cartels" that characterize capitalistic markets, wouldn't lead to "wealth concentration and the wage system, or to a corporate economy dominated by a small number of giant business organizations." Like the individualist anarchists of the late 19th century, Carson sees freed markets as a radically egalitarian force.

Carson's first interlocutor disagrees because "it is not enough to see corporations as purely a product of government intervention; there are additional powerful forces that tend to lead to market concentration." Offering his partly Marxist, partly Ostrom-ite, partly ecosocialist perspective, Derek Wall, the International Coordinator of the Green Party of England and Wales, humbly, but firmly, maintains "non-capitalist markets tend to lead to the restoration of capitalism." Despite disagreeing about the relationship of freed markets and corporate capitalism, Wall, who recently published *The Sustainable Economics of Elinor Ostrom:*

Commons, Contestation, and Craft, finds common ground with Kevin on the importance of self-governance.

Steve Horwitz, who's dabbled in the left-wing market anarchist debate before, takes on the role of sympathetic critic once again as the third participant in this month's Exchange. Dr. Horwitz is the Charles A. Dana Professor of Economics at St. Lawrence University in Canton, NY and author of the recently published *Hayek's Modern Family: Classical Liberalism and the Evolution of Social Institutions.* Horwitz's Bleeding-Heart Libertarianism can be seen in his charitable rebuttal to Carson's lead essay; but he ultimately concludes, "The problems with Carson's argument are the same ones that seem to infect much left-libertarian writing: too many assertions without careful economic argument about what a truly free market would look like and simultaneously overstating, in my view, the distortions created by the state by ignoring the underlying economics." But again, Carson's jousting partner finds common ground with him on the work of Elinor and Vincent Ostrom who "challenge the market/state dichotomy" and "force us to think more creatively about what a free society really means."

In Carson's rejoinders to Wall and Horwitz, he delves further into his intricate arguments to show why he believes both Wall and Horwitz still underestimate just how much state intervention distorts the market economy and turns it into one dominated by corporations and wage labor. While Carson takes the last word here, the discussion is far from over. Don't forget to check out October's *Mutual Exchange* to gain a better understanding of what a free market might look like and see the arguments from each perspective.

—*Cory Massimino, Mutual Exchange Coordinator, C4SS*

PART I

∞

Preliminary Work
on the
Subject
of
Economic Potentiality
&
Inevitability

CHAPTER

ONE

CAPITALISM: A GOOD WORD FOR A BAD THING

KEVIN CARSON

The Freeman editor Sheldon Richman, speaking at George Mason University, raised the question of just what mainstream libertarians mean when they call a country "capitalist." What qualifies a country as "capitalist"?

A lot of countries with relatively low indices of economic freedom (including those ranked as "mostly unfree") are conventionally regarded as "capitalist," and referred to as such in neoliberal agitprop comparing them favorably to non-capitalist countries like Cuba. And the talking heads at CNBC and scribblers in the business press commonly refer to "our capitalist system," even though it's doesn't even remotely approximate a free market.

So in common usage, among establishment libertarians

https://c4ss.org/content/1992

and what passes for mainstream "free market" wonks, any country that hasn't adopted Marxian socialism as its official ideology is "capitalist."

Based on these observations, Richman concludes that "capitalism" in practice "designates a system in which the means of production are de jure privately owned."

Interestingly, Murray Rothbard relates an anecdote in which Ludwig von Mises made that distinction, or something very like it, explicit. He asked Mises: Given that there's such a range of possible degrees of statism, from total statism to a totally free market, and given that no country approaches either absolute, what do you regard as the defining characteristic that divides essentially capitalist from essentially non-capitalist societies? Mises' response: The existence of a stock market. A society with a market for capital goods is essentially capitalist.

As I have pointed out in the past – a point Richman refers to in his address – it is rather odd that "capitalism" was adopted as the conventional term for a society based on private property and free exchange. There's no obvious reason, in seeking a name for an economy in which all factors of production are ostensibly equal and enter into free contract as equals, that capital should be singled in particular out for special emphasis. The choice of "capitalism" suggests some special ideological agenda, as if the system were run of, by and for capital as distinguished from other factors of production.

The unstated assumption embodied in calling a country "economically unfree" and yet capitalist, is this: An economically unfree country only ceases to be capitalist when the lack of economic freedom interferes with the ability of rich people to become richer from returns on land and capital. So long as the lack of economic freedom primarily limits the freedom of the poor to escape poverty, but the rich are able to enrich themselves on the pattern of UFC in Guatemala or Jack Abramoff's clients in the Marianas Islands, it's got the Good Housekeeping capitalist seal of approval.

Mises answer to Rothbard above – aside from confusing a "market for capital goods" with a market for equity in firms – implies that, no matter how economically unfree, a country in which most business enterprise is absentee-owned by the owners of concentrated wealth, and most labor is hired for wages by such absentee owners, passes muster as "capitalist." Presumably a country in which wealth was so widely distributed, and self-employment and cooperative ownership were such primary forms of social organization that stock trading was marginal in importance, would fall on the "socialist" side of Mises line–even if there were no regulatory constraints whatsoever on market exchange and the free movement of prices.

This is a very telling set of priorities: "capitalism," as opposed to "socialism," is not defined by the degree of economic freedom as such; it's defined by a particular institutional structure which is disproportionately to the benefit of a particular class of market actors.

As evidence that some forms of unfreedom matter more than others, consider the proclivity of some right-wingers for saying "Pinochet's political authoritarianism was lamentable, but at least he made Chile more free economically." Never mind "minor" issues like whether reversing a land reform and returning land from the people who worked it to a landed oligarchy was a step toward "economic freedom."

Just consider Pinochet's authoritarian suppression of the labor movement: Had it been the owners of capital, and not the sellers of labor-power, who had been tortured and disappeared, or found in ditches with their faces hacked off, I doubt they would have said the same thing. It's an odd distinction to treat repression of the owners of one factor of production as economic, but of the owners of another factor as only "political." This assumption underlies most mainstream "free market" commentary in the business press and business news channels: Even when they explicitly refer to "our free market system" in so many words, they really mean a system in which most business enterprise is nominally "private." No matter how statist a system of regulations is in effect, so long as they're exercised primarily through "private" actors, and most money passes through the hands of such "private" actors rather than the U.S. Treasury, it's a "free market" system. Hence, the kind of "free market" agenda you see at places like Heritage and the Adam Smith Institute for "privatizing" government functions by contracting them out to "private businesses," even when those businesses are guaranteed a profit at taxpayer expense.

And by the way, those who object to all this as a form of semantic gamesmanship should remember that Mises and Rand were responsible, from the 1920s on, for the deliberate rehabilitation of "capitalism" as a term of pro-market apologetics. Before Mises' time, "capitalism" was used by mainstream political economists to describe the actual system of political economy they lived under–i.e., historic capitalism.

"Capitalism," simply put, is the most honest term for the unfree market we live under. It's a system of, by and for the owners of capital; so long as it retains that primary characteristic, it's "capitalist," no matter how unfree the market.

CHAPTER
TWO

BIG BUSINESS AND THE RISE OF AMERICAN STATISM

ROY A. CHILDS

Preface

This essay constitutes a part of "revisionism" in history, largely domestic history. The term revisionism originally came into use referring to historiography after World War I. A group of young historians, eager to uncover the realities behind the blanket of myths surrounding the origins of this crucial conflict, discovered as a result of their investigations that Germany and Austria were not, contrary to popular mythology, solely responsible for the outbreak of that crisis. Thus, reevaluating the history of the immediate past, these historians came to see the Treaty of Versailles, forced upon the losers of that war, as monstrously unjust, and maintained

Reason (magazine), 1971; https://c4ss.org/content/12431

that the rigid enforcement of its terms would lead to further world conflict. They came to advocate a radical overhauling and revision of the Versailles Treaty — whence the term "revisionism."

Since then, revisionism has been applied to virtually any renegade school of thought in historiography that took issue with the "official government line" on important events in history. As it is used today, revisionism is a general concept subsuming a wide variety of schools, or integrating conceptions of man's past. For at the time when any set of events occurs, in any context, there is almost always a specific set of interpretations of events, a given historical paradigm, which spreads throughout a given culture to the relative exclusion of other interpretations.

Those schools of historiography that are responsible for refuting the popular myths, for revising the historical record in accordance with new evidence, are thus called revisionist in nature. In this preface, it is my intention to sketch briefly what I consider to be the nature and status of history as a field of investigation. I want especially to focus on the crucially important, yet neglected, relationship of philosophy to history. In the nineteenth century, practically every great philosopher made extensive use of history, particularly in fields such as social philosophy; and, every great historian was usually well acquainted with philosophy. Yet today historians and philosophers often seem to be completely cut off from one another. This is unfortunate, for history is vitally important to the philosopher, at the very least in illustrating his theories, in filling in the outlines of an abstract theory with concrete units and events. Similarly, philosophy is critically important to history in at least two interrelated ways: philosophy necessarily serves as a critic, and a guide, on two important levels — methodology, and evaluation. No one who deals with questions of responsibility, causality, or even the problem of "knowing" concrete events to which the human mind no longer has direct access through immediate awareness (as opposed to inference), can escape the importance of philosophy.

But the problem is more complicated than that. Today, certain philosophers tend to dismiss specific social theories, such as libertarianism and laissez-faire, almost out-of-hand, usually because of alleged historical figures regarding centralization of economic power, depressions, unemployment, imperialism, war and so forth. And certain historians (usually those operating from an implicit philosophic base such as Marxism), in an attempt to pump "relevance" into history, insist on drawing explicitly nonhistorical conclusions from purely historical data. Thus, such key revisionist authors as Gabriel Kolko and William Appleman Williams often mention in the course of their historical studies that such-and-such was "a necessary consequence of American capitalism." Aside from the enormous problems involved in the question of "necessity" as such in all fields, surely we face here more than a strictly historic judgment! At the barest minimum, such a statement would put the responsibility of proof on the shoulders of the proponent, who must marshal not only historical data, but economic theory and social philosophy as well — not to mention epistemology, which alone can provide him with a systematic methodology. Notice this intricate statement in Joyce and Gabriel Kolko's masterly The Limits of Power: "A society's goals, in the last analysis, reflect its objective needs — economic, strategic, and political — in the light of the requirements of its very specific structure of power." This is certainly not a strictly historical judgment. These questions immediately arise: What does it mean to talk of a "society's" goals? What are a "society's objective needs, and how does one determine them? What are the "requirements" of a specific structure of power, and what is meant here by the term "specific structure of power"? The point is not to fall back on agnosticism and skepticism, but to raise the question of whether or not such questions can be answered — or even raised — from within the context of history alone. If they cannot be, then we obviously fall into such fields as economics and philosophy. But philosophy first: it is only philosophy that, properly speaking, will give us the means of answering the very question of whether or not such-and-such a problem can be answered by historical inquiry alone.

Although I have stressed the dependence of history on philosophy, I do not mean to imply that history is merely tangential to philosophy. The philosopher, in my view, should, if nothing else, regard history as a testing ground, an experimental laboratory in which he conceptually can apply his theories (particularly social and political theories, and ethics) in an attempt to see if they make sense. A philosopher who preaches total state control of individual human actions and decisions, for instance, might profitably look at history for instances of what has happened as his ideal has been approached, approached as a limit case. If he finds destruction, chaos and the like, then the burden of explaining this within the confines of his assertions of the supposedly beneficial nature of state control comes into play. Similarly, if an advocate of laissez-faire holds that depressions are impossible or unlikely in a free market economy, then he must be prepared to explain the nature and genesis of historical depressions by another theory than the prevalent ones, and to call into play historical data which other schools either neglect or misinterpret. Finally, the philosopher can profitably regard historical evaluations and interpretations as practice for actually applying his theories in interpreting contemporary events.

Since space does not permit me to detail every major issue in the philosophy of history, I shall restrict myself to presenting some of the more interesting points which a developed philosophy of history should focus on. And within these limits, I shall summarize my own approaches to some key problem areas.

What is history? History is a selective recreation of the events of the past, according to a historian's premises regarding what is important and his judgment concerning the nature of causality in human action. This selectivity is a most important aspect of history, and it is this alone which prevents history from becoming a random chronicling of events. And since this selectivity is necessary to history, the only remaining question is whether or not such judgments will be made explicitly or implicitly, with full knowledge of what one considers to be important and why, or without such awareness. Selection presupposes a means, method, or principle of selection. The historian's view of the nature of causality in human action also is determined by a principle of selection. He can have a conscious theory, such as economic determinism, or attempt to function without one. But without one, the result of historical investigation is likely to appear disintegrated and patched together. In this case, the historian depends necessarily on philosophy, on economics and on psychology. If he is not aware of his selections and presuppositions, then the result is a bad historian, or at best a confused one. Charles A. Beard was more self-conscious than most about the problems of historical method, yet he still could write, at the apex of his career, an essay entitled "Written History as an Act of Faith." Of philosophical evasion and bankruptcy are bad historians born, as are professionals in so many other fields. A professional in any field has the unshakable responsibility to be aware of and name his primaries, those presuppositions which function as axiomatic in his field. If he intends to be taken seriously, then he should be prepared to defend them. Evasion on any level produces disastrous consequences for man; on the highest political and intellectual levels, evasion can result in such things as physical destruction, or in entire generations of scholars being misled in their scholarly pursuits.

A popular philosophical doctrine holds that the methodology of history is entirely different from the methodology of other sciences. Yet fundamentally the methodology of all sciences is the same — logic. The nature of the evidence relevant to one field may differ from that relevant to another, and this indeed accounts for the apparent differences of method. Yet truths in any field are in fact verified by a process of applying man's reason to objective evidence. By "reason" I mean simply the faculty of integrated awareness which is responsible for all of man's knowledge above the perceptual level; by "objective evidence" I mean reality as presented to the intellect — "objective" meaning that which is determined by the nature of the entities existing in reality, and "evidence" referring to that context or "segment" of reality which a consciousness has become aware of. The nature of the objective evidence which is largely considered in history is simply human testimony, direct or indirect. History as a field deals with past human thought and actions. Since we have no direct awareness of the contents of anyone's consciousness but our own, we must rely on inference from what a person says, and what he does. Considered from a different perspective, history deals with the ends that men have held in the past, and the means that they have adopted to attain these ends. Since no two individuals are specifically alike in every particular characteristic, it is impossible to recreate the past in the form of a laboratory experiment and to observe the effects of single causal factors on human action. Thus, all that one can do is to collect evidence concerning the context of individual men, their ideas and their actions, using a theory or model of the nature of causality in human action that interprets or selectively reconstructs events of the past, omitting what one judges to be unimportant, and offering an explanation for what one does consider to be important, in light of the evidence available. Utopian "completeness" is neither possible nor necessary in knowledge — in history or anywhere else. All knowledge is contextual, but this does not in any way hinder knowledge from being valid.

Turning from this sketch of historical method, I shall indicate, briefly, the value of history. Traditionalists often seek to use history as a guide to action, spurning abstract guides to conduct provided by the science of ethics, and adopting conventions and traditions instead. Yet it should be noted at the outset that to use history in any reasonable way to find rules of conduct presupposes a rational ethic. One must use a rational ethic to differentiate "good" traditions from bad, and in fact to supersede history altogether in projecting what is possible to man. If something has happened in history, then one rationally can conclude that it is possible for man; if something has not happened in history, the reverse is not true — one cannot conclude that it is not possible for man. History can illustrate principles, but cannot verify or refute them. It is important to point out the submission of history to a rational ethic in this regard.

People distraught with the present often seek stability and refuge in the past, idealizing it beyond recognition. Such an attitude, however, will only lead to a life built on illusions, to despair that tomorrow things will only be worse, and a general feeling of impotence and inefficacy, with the result that those who accept such a view will not act to attain a better future.

But to act to change things for the better presupposes not only that one understands a rational ethic and its principles, but that one has some idea of "where one is," historically speaking. One has to answer the question: what is the present context of man? To answer this takes a knowledge of what ends men have sought up to now, in a broad cultural and political sense, and what means they have adopted to attain them. One then applies the principles of a rational philosophy to his actions; understanding his context, he acts to change things in a certain direction.

If either history or philosophy, specifically, ethics, is left out of this, an ideology is necessarily incomplete. On the one hand there is the error of those who, like William Appleman Williams, "are committed to the proposition that History is the most consequential way of learning who we are and what we should do." On the other hand, there is the fallacy of those who develop a social philosophy and attempt to apply it without any knowledge of what is going on in the world.

In response to Williams, it can be said that history cannot tell us "what we should do." At best, it can pinpoint problems which people historically have faced, and solutions which they have attempted to apply.

In response to the others, it should be stated that the application of the most consistent philosophy to real events requires a journalistic knowledge of the state of the world. This differentiates ideology from philosophy. Whereas philosophy abstracts from time, and hence from history, the fundamental truths about man and his relationship to reality, ideology is a consistent world view. It integrates philosophy with one's context, applies the principles of philosophy to the concrete realities of the world. Philosophy is concerned with the nature and validity of human knowledge, with validating and detailing the precepts of a rational ethic with truth. Ideology is concerned with applying philosophy to any given historical context — with making truth relevant, which comes from an integrated focus on man as he is in any historical context.

The transition from philosophy to ideology is largely accomplished by history. To use an analogy, philosophy discovers a rational ethic, but every given individual must apply its precepts to his own life by identifying the context he faces and making concrete choices by means of logic. The "major premise" in this version of the Aristotelian "practical syllogism" is the ethical premise itself. The "minor premise" is the concrete in anyone's life which the principles subsume. The "conclusion" is the action to be taken. Similarly in the transition from philosophy to ideology, the major premise is the ethical-philosophic principle; the minor premises are the concrete details, or "existential premises" summarizing some aspect of the context of man in some historical period. The conclusion is the ideological stand to be taken.

It is important to emphasize the overwhelming necessity of having a valid existential premise in either the individual or the general case. In ideology, invalid historical or existential premises can make the stand taken totally inconsistent with the basic thrust of the philosophy which generated it initially. The result of errors may be that the ideological stand ends up on the wrong side of the fence.

Now a word on some of my own positions on basic issues. Believing that the universe consists of a number of distinct entities which are related to each other by both real and mental relations (having an objective foundation in fact), I hold that things necessarily act in accordance with their individual natures, producing results in accordance with such natures. Concepts and theories are therefore formed by integrating particulars according to common characteristics into new mental entities.

In history, I hold that events consist of the actions of individuals motivated toward certain ends and using certain means to attain them. But since individuals often have the same values and conceptions of appropriate means to attain their ends, they often work together. In fact, the whole function of institutions is to enable individual human actions to be systematically and consciously integrated in producing common ends. It is this fact which gives rise to all classifications and hence all "class analysis." "Classes" in social theory, or political theory, or historical investigation, must of necessity be groups of individuals having common characteristics. It is my view that man has free will, and that the concept and existence of free will is a necessary postulate if an obvious fact of man's nature is to be explained: his capacity for conceptual and propositional speech, and his ability to identify facts of reality. Determinism, in the strict sense, is contradictory. For if a man's mental processes — specifically, his attempts at reasoning — are not free, if they are determined by environment and heredity, then there is no means of claiming that theory x is true is true and y is false — since man can have no way of knowing that his mental processes might not be conditioned to force him to believe that x is logical, when in fact it is not.

This means that "classes" in history are not primarily economic, in the usual sense of the term, but rather, are *ethical.* Man is not born with values, or preferences except on a sensory level (pleasure or pain), and he does not merely absorb values from a culture like a sponge absorbs water. Rather, men must *choose* their values, by intention or default. And the realm of chosen values is the realm of ethics. This belief in ethical classes is the *root* of my disagreement with Marxism.

A related fallacy of Marxism, especially in relation to its effect in guiding historical investigation, is its simplistic conception of what constitutes a class "interest." "Interests" are not primary, nor automatic. Apart from that category of things which actually benefit men (whether or not men are aware of them) "interests" can only be arrived at through a process of consciousness; evaluation. This means that, given an objective standard of the organism's life and well-being, a given man's values and conception of his own or his "class's" interests can be right or wrong. More importantly, classes are derived from and validated by reference to concrete individuals, actions and values, not vice versa. Classifications are derived from things, not vice versa.

This is important to focus on for a moment. For Marx, despite all his anti-Idealistic and anti-Hegelian rhetoric, is really an Idealist and Hegelian on the issue of classification. Whatever attempts he makes to get around this point, Marx is still asserting, at root, that a classification (a social class) precedes and determines the characteristic of those who are members or units of the classification. Marx is, in fact, very unclear on the nature of the exact process of causation which occurs in the interaction between those people who own the "means of production," their ideas ("interests") and actions, and those people relating to them. Since any such theory of causality in human action is vitally important in historical investigation, it is to be expected that Marxism corrupts historical investigation.

Interestingly enough, this is very relevant to the subject of this essay: the role of big business in promoting American statism. For if nothing else, this essay shows that the "class lines" in American history are different from what they were thought to be. Some of the men in larger businesses supported and even initiated acts of government regulation while others, particularly relatively smaller and more competent competitors, opposed such regulation. Thus we have a clear-cut case in American history that contradicts Marxian theory: the lines of battle and conflict were not drawn merely over the issue and criterion of individuals' relation to the means of production, but on much more complicated grounds. A better classification might be along the lines set down by Franz Oppenheimer: the state-benefited and the state-oppressed — those who gained their wealth by means of confiscation, robbery and restriction of other people's noncoercive activities, and those who gained their wealth by means of free trade in a free market, by the method of voluntary exchange. But even here the lines are not clear-cut, and we find cases of those who were honest producers sanctioning theft and parasitism, as well as cases of those who were parasites and benefiters from statism opposing controls — twin cases of hypocrisy and altruism.

Needless to add, many contemporary Marxists have responded to the challenge with ever new wings being added on to classical Marxist theory to "explain," in an ad hoc fashion, the events which do not fit into classic Marxist paradigms.

Historically, whenever defenders of some classic paradigm, in any field, begin to confront problems which conflict with the basic theory, they begin increasingly to modify the particulars of the theory to conform to fact without ever questioning the basic paradigm itself. But sooner or later any such imitation of the path taken by the followers of Ptolemy must end in the same way: the paradigm will collapse and be replaced by a new paradigm which explains all the known facts in a much simpler manner, thus conforming to a fundamental rule of scientific methodology: Occam's razor. The new paradigm, I think, will be the paradigm of libertarianism.

The purpose of this particular essay is simply to apply some of the principles of libertarianism to an interpretation of events in a very special and important period of human history. I have attempted to give a straightforward summary of New Left revisionist findings in one area of domestic history: the antitrust movement and Progressive Era. But I have done so not as a New Leftist, not as a historian proper, but as a libertarian, that is, a social philosopher of a specific school.

In doing this summary, I have two interrelated purposes: first, to show Objectivists and Libertarians that certain of their beliefs in history are wrong and need to be revised under the impact of new evidence, and simultaneously to illustrate to them a specific means of approaching historical problems, to identify one cause of the growth of American statism and to indicate a new way of looking at history. Secondly, my purpose is to show New Left radicals that far from undermining the position of laissez-faire capitalism (as opposed to what they call state capitalism, a system of government controls which is not yet socialism in the classic sense), their historical discoveries actually support the case for a totally free market. Then, too, I wish to illustrate how a libertarian would respond to the problems raised by New Left historians. Finally, I wish implicitly to apply Occam's razor by showing that there is a simpler explanation of events than that so often colored with Marxist theory. Without exception, Marxist postulates are not necessary to explain the facts of reality.

Conflicting Schools of Thought

In historiography different schools of thought exist in much the same way and for the same reason as in many other fields. And in history, as in those other fields, different interpretations, no matter how far removed from reality, tend to go on forever, oblivious to new evidence and theories. In his book, The Structure of Scientific Revolutions, Thomas Kuhn shows in the physical sciences how an existing paradigm of scientific explanation tends to ignore new evidence and theories, being overthrown only when: (a) the puzzles and problems generated by a false paradigm pile up to an increasingly obvious extent, so that an ever-wider range of material cannot be integrated into the paradigm, and an ever-growing number of problems cannot be solved, and (b) there arises on the scene a new paradigm to replace the old.

In history, perhaps more than in most other fields, the criteria of truth have not been sufficiently developed, resulting in a great number of schools of thought that tend to rise and fall in influence more because of political and cultural factors than because of epistemological factors. The result also has been that in history there are a number of competing paradigms to explain different sets of events, all connected to specific political views. In this essay, I shall consider three of them: the Marxist view, the conservative view and the liberal view. I shall examine how these paradigms function with reference to one major area of American history — the Progressive Era — and with respect to one major issue: the roots of government regulation of the economy, particularly through the antitrust laws and the Federal Reserve System. Other incidents will also be mentioned, but this issue will be the focus.

Among these various schools, nearly everyone agrees on the putative facts of American history; disagreements arise over frameworks of interpretation and over evaluation. The Marxists, liberals, and conservatives all agree that in the economic history of America in the nineteenth century, the facts were roughly as follows. After midcentury, industrialization proceeded apace in America, as a consequence of the laissez-faire policies pursued by the United States government, resulting in increasing centralization and concentration of economic power.

According to the liberal, in the nineteenth century there was an individualistic social system in the United States, which, when left unchecked, led inevitably to the "strong" using the forces of a free market to smash and subdue the "weak," by building gigantic, monopolistic industrial enterprises which dominated and controlled the life of the nation. Then, as this centralization proceeded to snowball, the "public" awoke to its impeding subjugation at the hands of these monopolistic businessmen. The public was stirred by the injustice of it all and demanded reform, whereupon altruistic and far-seeing politicians moved quickly to mash the monopolists with antitrust laws and other regulation of the economy, on behalf of the ever-suffering "little man" who was saved thereby from certain doom. Thus did the American government squash the greedy monopolists and restore competition, equality of opportunity and the like, which was perishing in the unregulated laissez-faire free market economy. Thus did the American state act to save both freedom and capitalism.

The Marxists also hold that there was in fact a trend toward centralization of the economy at the end of the last century, and that this was inherent in the nature of capitalism as an economic system. (Some modern, more sophisticated Marxists maintain, on the contrary, that historically the state was always involved in the so-called capitalistic economy.) Different Marxists see the movement towards state regulation of the economy in different ways. One group basically sees state regulation as a means of prolonging the collapse of the capitalistic system, a means which they see as inherently unstable. They see regulation as an attempt by the ruling class to deal with the "inner contradictions" of capitalism. Another group, more sophisticated, sees the movement towards state regulation as a means of hastening the cartelization and monopolization of the economy under the hands of the ruling class.

The conservative holds, like the liberal, that there was indeed such a golden age of individualism, when the economy was almost completely free of government controls. But far from being evil, such a society was near-utopian in their eyes. But the government intervened and threw things out of kilter. The consequence was that the public began to clamor for regulation in order to rectify things that were either not injustices at all, or were injustices imposed by initial state actions. The antitrust laws and other acts of state interference, by this view, were the result. But far from seeing the key large industrialists and bankers as monopolistic monsters, the conservatives defend them as heroic innovators who were the victims of misguided or power-lusting progressives who used big businessmen as scapegoats and sacrifices on the altar of the "public good." All three of the major schools of interpretation of this crucial era in American history hold two premises in common: (a) that the trend in economic organization at the end of the nineteenth century was in fact towards growing centralization of economic power, and (b) that this trend was an outcome of the processes of the free market. Only the Marxists, and then only a portion of them, take issue with the additional premise that the actions of state regulation were anti-big business in motivation, purpose and results. And both the conservatives and the liberals see a sharp break between the ideas and men involved in the Progressive Movement and those of key big business and financial leaders. Marxists disagree with many of these views, but hold the premise that the regulatory movement itself was an outgrowth of the capitalistic economy.

The Marxists, of course, smuggle in specifically non-historical conclusions and premises, based on their wider ideological frame of reference, the most prominent being the idea of necessity applied to historical events.

Although there are many arguments and disputes between adherents of the various schools, none of the schools has disputed the fundamental historical premise that the dominant trend at the end of the last century was toward increasing centralization of the economy, or the fundamental economic premise that this alleged increase was the result of the operations of a laissez-faire free market system.

Yet there are certain flaws in all three interpretations, flaws that are both historical and theoretical, flaws that make any of the interpretations inadequate, necessitating a new explanation. Although it is not possible here to argue in depth against the three interpretations, brief reasons for their inadequacy can be given.

Aside from the enormous disputes in economics over questions such as whether or not the "capitalistic system" inherently leads toward concentration and centralization of economic power in the hands of a few, we can respond to the Marxists, as well as to others, by directing our attention to the premise that there was in fact economic centralization at the turn of the century. In confronting the liberals, once more we can begin by pointing to the fact that there has been much more centralization since the Progressive Era than before, and that the function, if not the alleged purpose, of the antitrust and other regulatory laws has been to increase, rather than decrease, such centralization. Since the conservatives already question, on grounds of economic theory, the premise that the concentration of economic power results inevitably from a free market system, we must question them as to why they believe that (a) a free market actually existed during the period in question, and (b) how, then, such centralization of economic power resulted from this supposed free market.

Aside from all the economic arguments, let us look at the period in question to see if any of the schools presented hold up, in any measure or degree.

The Roots of Regulation

In fact and in history, the entire thesis of all three schools is botched, from beginning to end. The interpretations of the Marxists, the liberals and the conservatives are a tissue of lies.

As Gabriel Kolko demonstrates in his masterly The Triumph of Conservatism and in Railroads and Regulation, the dominant trend in the last three decades of the nineteenth century and the first two of the twentieth was not towards increasing centralization, but rather, despite the growing number of mergers and the growth in the overall size of many corporations,

> toward growing competition. Competition was unacceptable to many key business and financial leaders, and the merger movement was to a large extent a

> reflection of voluntary, unsuccessful business efforts to bring irresistible trends under control. ... As new competitors sprang up, and as economic power was diffused throughout an expanding nation, it became apparent to many important businessmen that only the national government could [control and stabilize] the economy. ... Ironically, contrary to the consensus of historians, it was not the existence of monopoly which caused the federal government to intervene in the economy, but the lack of it.[1]

While Kolko does not consider the causes and context of the economic crises which faced businessmen from the 1870s on, we can at least summarize some of the more relevant aspects here. The enormous role played by the state in American history has not yet been fully investigated by anyone. Those focusing on the role of the federal government in regulating the economy often neglect to mention the fact that America's ostensive federalist system means that the historian concerned with the issue of regulation must look to the various state governments as well. What he will find already has been suggested by a growing number of historians: that nearly every federal program was pioneered by a number of state governments, including subsidies, land grants and regulations of the antitrust variety. Furthermore, often neglected in these accounts is the fact that the real process of centralization of the economy came not during the Progressive Era, but rather (initially) during the Civil War, with its immense alliance between the state and business (at least in the more industrialized North). Indeed, such

[1]Gabriel Kolko, *The Triumph of Conservatism* (Chicago: Quadrangle Publishing Co., 1967), pp. 4-5.

key figures in the progressive Era as J. P. Morgan got their starts in alliances with the government of the North in the Civil War. The Civil War also saw the greatest inflationary expansion of the monetary supply and greatest land grants to the railroads in American history. These and other related facts mean that an enormous amount of economic malinvestment occurred during and immediately after the Civil War, and the result was that a process of liquidation of malinvestment took place: a depression in the 1870s.

It was this process of inflationary book caused by the banking and credit system spurred by the government and followed by depressions, that led the businessmen and financial leaders to seek stabilizing elements from the 1870s on. One of the basic results of this process of liquidation, of course, was a growth in competition. The thesis of the Kolko books is that the trend was towards growing competition in the United States before the federal government intervened, and that various big businessmen in different fields found themselves unable to cope with this trend by private, economic means. Facing falling profits and diffusion of economic power, these businessmen then turned to the state to regulate the economy on their behalf. What Kolko and his fellow revisionist James Weinstein (*The Corporate Ideal in the Liberal State, 1900-1918*) maintain is that business and financial leaders did not merely react to these situations with concrete proposals for regulations, but with the ever more sophisticated development of a comprehensive ideology which embraced both foreign and domestic policy. Weinstein in particular links up the process of businessmen turning to the state for favors in response to problems which they faced and the modern "corporate liberal" system. he maintains that the ideology now dominant in the U.S. had been worked out for the most part by the end of the First World War, not during the New Deal, as is commonly held, and that the "ideal of a liberal corporate social order" was developed consciously and purposefully by those who then, as now, enjoyed supremacy in the United States: "the more sophisticated leaders of America's largest corporations and financial institutions."[2] In examining this thesis, I shall focus predominantly on the activities of the national Civics Federation (NCF), a group of big businessmen that was the primary ideological force behind many "reforms."

Since the basic pattern of regulation was first established in the case of the railroads, a glance at this industry will set the basis for an examination of the others. American industry as a whole was intensely competitive in the period from 1875 on. Many industries, including the railroads, had over-expanded and were facing a squeeze on profits. American history contains the myth that the railroads faced practically no competition at all during this period, that freight rates constantly rose, pinching every last penny out of the shippers, especially the farmers, and bleeding them to death. Historian Kolko shows that:

> Contrary to the common view, railroad freight rates, taken as a whole, declined almost continuously over the period [from 1877 to 1916] and although consolidation of railroads proceeded apace, this phenomenon never affected the long-term decline of rates or the ultimately competitive nature of much of the industry. In their desire to establish stability

[2] James Weinstein, *The Corporate Ideal in the Liberal State* (Boston: Beacon Press, 1968), p. ix.

> and control over rates and competition, the railroads often resorted to voluntary, cooperative efforts.
>
> When these efforts failed, as they inevitably did, the railroad men turned to political solutions to [stabilize] their increasingly chaotic industry. They advocated measures designed to bring under control those railroads within their own ranks that refused to conform to voluntary compacts. ... [F]rom the beginning of the 20th century until at least the initiation of World War I, the railroad industry resorted primarily to political alternatives and gave up the abortive efforts to put its own house in order by relying on voluntary cooperation. ... Insofar as the railroad men did think about the larger theoretical implications of centralized federal regulation, they rejected ... the entire notion of laissez-faire [and] most railroad leaders increasingly relied on a Hamiltonian conception of the national government.[3]

The two major means used by competitors to cut into each other's markets were rate wars (price cutting) and rebates; the aim of business leaders was to stop these. Their major, unsuccessful, tool was the "pool" which was continuously broken up by competitive factors.[4] The first serious pooling effort in the East, sponsored by the New York Central, had been tried as early as 1874 by Vanderbilt; the pool

[3]Gabriel Kolko, *Railroads and Regulation* (Princeton: Princeton University Press, 1965), pp. 3-5.

[4]See both Kolko books for factual proof of this. Weinstein does not take this fact into account in his book, and thus underestimates this as a motivating force in the actions and beliefs of businessmen. For a theoretical explanation, see Murray N. Rothbard, *Man, Economy and State* (Los Angeles: Nash Publishing Co, 1971), II pp. 566-585. (See also, Chapter 10, Section 2: Cartels and Their Consequences.)

lasted for six months. In September 1876,a Southwestern Railroad Association was formed by seven major companies in an attempt to voluntarily enforce a pool; it didn't work and collapsed in early 1878. Soon it became obvious to most industrial leaders that the pooling system was ineffective.

In 1876 the first significant federal regulatory bill was introduced into the House by J. R. Hopkins of Pittsburgh. Drawn up by the attorney for the Philadelphia and Reading Railroad, it died in committee.

By 1879, there was "a general unanimity among pool executives ... that without government sanctions, the railroads would never maintain or stabilize rates."[5] By 1880, the railroads were in serious trouble; the main threat was identified as "cutthroat competition."

Far from pushing the economy toward greater centralization, economic forces indicated that centralization was inefficient and unstable. The push was towards decentralization, and smaller railroads often found themselves much less threatened by economic turns of events than the older, more established and larger business concerns.

Thus the Marxist model finds itself seriously in jeopardy in this instance, for the smaller forms and railroads, throughout the crises of the 1870s and 1880s often were found to be making larger profits on capital invested than the giant businesses. Furthermore, much of the concentration of economic power which was apparent during the 1870s and on, was the result of massive state aid immediately before, during, and after the Civil War, not the result of free market forces. Much of the capital accumulation — particularly in the cases of the railroads and banks — was accomplished by means of

[5]Kolko, *Railroads*, p. 26.

government regulation and aid, not by free trade on a free market.

Also, the liberal and conservative models which stress the supposed fact that there was growing centralization in the economy and that competition either lessened or became less intense, are both shaken by historical facts. And we already have seen that it was the railroad leaders, faced with seemingly insurmountable problems, who initiated the drive for federal government regulation of their industry.

Rate wars during 1881 pushed freight rates down 50 percent between July and October alone; between 1882 and 1886, freight rates declined for the nation as a whole by 20 percent. Railroads were increasingly talking about regulation with a certain spark of interest. Chauncey Depew, attorney for the New York Central, had become convinced "of the [regulatory commission's] necessity ... for the protection of both the public and the railroads.[6] He soon converted William H. Vanderbilt to his position.[7]

Agitation for regulation to ease competitive pains increased, and in 1887, the Interstate Commerce Act was passed. According to the Railway Review, an organ of the railroad, it was only a first step.

The Act was not enough, and it did not stop either the rate wars or rebates. So, early in 1889 during a prolonged rate war, J. P. Morgan summoned presidents of major railroads to New York to find ways to maintain rates and enforce

[6]Kolko, *Railroads*, p. 17.

[7]The twin facts here that Vanderbilt needed "converting" and that he had other options open to him should by themselves put to rest the more *simplistic* Marxist theories of "class consciousness," awareness of interests and relationships to the means of production.

the act, but this, too, was a failure. The larger railroads were harmed most by this competition; the smaller railroads were in many cases more prosperous than in the early 1880s. "Morgan weakened rather than strengthened many of his roads ... [and on them] services and safety often declined. Many of Morgan's lines were overexpanded into areas where competition was already too great."[8] Competition again increased. The larger roads then led the fight for further regulation, seeking more power for the Interstate Commerce Commission (ICC).

In 1891, the president of a midwestern railroad advocated that the entire matter of setting rates be turned over to the ICC. An ICC poll taken in 1892 of fifteen railroads showed that fourteen of them favored legalized pooling under Commission control. Another important businessman, A. A. Walker, who zipped back and forth betwene business and government agencies, said that "railroad men had had enough of competition. The phrase 'free competition' sounds well enough as a universal regulator," he said, "but it regulates by the knife."[9]

In 1906, the Hepburn Act was passed, also with business backing. The railroad magnate Cassatt spoke out as a major proponent of the act and said that he had long endorsed federal rate regulation. Andrew Carnegie, too, popped up to endorse the act. George W. Perkins, an important Morgan associate, wrote his boss that the act "is going to work out for the ultimate and great good of the railroad." But such controls were not enough for some big businessmen. Thus E. P. Ripley, the president of the Santa Fe, suggested what

[8]Kolko, *Railroads*, pp. 65-66.

[9]Kolko, *Railroads*, p. 74.

amounted to a Federal Reserve System for the railroads, cheerfully declaring that such a system "would do away with the enormous wastes of the competitive system, and permit business to follow the line of least resistance" — a chant later taken up by Mussolini.

In any case, we have seen that (a) the trend was not towards centralization at the close of the nineteenth century — rather, the liquidation of previous malinvestment fostered by state action and bank-led inflation worked against the bigger businesses in favor of the smaller, less overextended businesses; (b) there was, in the case of the railroads anyway, no sharp dichotomy or antagonism between big businessmen and the progressive Movement's thrust for regulation; and (c) the purpose of the regulations, as seen by key business leaders, was not to fight the growth of "monopoly" and centralization, but to foster it.

The culmination of this big-business-sponsored "reform" of the economic system is actually today's system. The new system took effect immediately during world War I when railroads gleefully handed over control to the government in exchange for guaranteed rate increases and guaranteed profits, something continued under the Transportation Act of 1920. The consequences, of course, are still making themselves felt, as in 1971, when the Pennsylvania Railroad, having cut itself off from the market and from market calculation nearly entirely, was found to be in a state of economic chaos. It declared bankruptcy and later was rescued, in part, by the state.

Regulation Comes to the Rest of the Economy

Having illustrated my basic thesis through a case study of the origins of regulation in the railroad industry, I shall now look at the rest of the American economy in this period and examine, however briefly, the role that big business had in pushing through acts of state regulation.

I should also mention, at least in passing, big businessmen not only had a particularly important effect in pushing through domestic regulation, but they fostered interventionism in foreign policy as well. What was common to both spheres was the fact that the acts of state intervention and monetary expansion by the state-manipulated banking system had precipitated depressions and recessions from the 1870s though the 1890s. The common response of businessmen, particularly big businessmen — the leaders in various fields — was to promote further state regulation and aid as a solution to the problems caused by the depressions. In particular vogue at the time — in vogue today, as a matter of fact — was the notion that continued American prosperity required (as a necessary condition) expanded markets for American goods and manufactured items. This led businessmen to seek markets in foreign lands though various routes, having fulfilled their "manifest destiny" at home.

Domestically, however, the immediate result was much more obvious. From about 1875 on, many corporations, wishing to be large and dominant in their field, over-expanded and over-capitalized. Mediocre entrepreneurship, administrative difficulties and increasing competition cut deeply into the markets and profits of many giants. Mergers often were tried, as in the railroad industry, but the larger mergers brought neither greater profits nor less competition. As Kolko states: "Quite the opposite occurred. There was more competition, and profits, if anything, declined." A survey of ten mergers showed, for instance, that the companies earned an average of 65 percent of their preconsolidation profits after consolidation. Over-centralization inhibited their flexibility of action, and hence their ability to respond to changing market conditions. In short, things were not as bad for other industries as for the railroads – they were often worse.

In the steel industry, the price of most steel goods declined more or less regularly until 1895, and even though prices rose somewhat thereafter, there was considerable insecurity about what other competitors might choose to do next. A merger of many corporations in 1901, based on collaboration between Morgan and Carnegie, resulted in the formation of U. S. Steel. Yet U.S. Steel's profit margin declined over 50 percent between 1902 and 1904. In its first two decades of existence, U. S. Steel held a continually shrinking share of the market. Due to technological conservatism and inflexible leadership, the company became increasingly costly and inefficient. Voluntary efforts at control failed. U. S. Steel turned to politics.

In the oil industry, where Standard Oil was dominant, the same situation existed. In 1899 there were 67 petroleum refiners in the U.S.; within ten years, the number had grown to 147 refiners.

In the telephone industry, things were in a similar shape. From its foundation in 1877 until 1894, Bell Telephone (AT&T) had a virtual monopoly in the industry based on its control of almost all patents.[10] In 1894 many of the patents expired. "Bell immediately adopted a policy of harassing the host of aspiring competitors by suing them (27 suits were instituted in 1894-95 alone) for allegedly infringing Bell patents."[11] But such efforts to stifle competition failed; by 1902, there were 9,100 independent telephone systems; by 1907, there were 22,000. Most had rates lower than AT&T.

In the meat packing industry too, the large packers felt threatened by increasing competition. Their efforts at control failed. Similar diffusion of economic power was the case in other fields, such as banking, where the power of the eastern financiers was being seriously eroded by midwestern competitors.

This, then, was the basic context of big business; these were the problems that it faced. How did it react? Almost unanimously, it turned to the power of the state to get what it could not get by voluntary means. Big business acted not only through concrete political pressure, but by engaging in large-scale, long-run ideological propaganda or "education" aimed at getting different sections of the American society united behind statism, in principle and practice.

Let us look at some of the activities of the major organizational tool of big business, the National Civics Federation. The NCF was actually a reincarnation of Hamiltonian views

---

[10]It is instructive to note that most of these patents were illegitimate according to libertarian ownership theories, since many other men had independently discovered the telephone and subsequent items besides Bell and the AT&T group, yet they were coercively restrained from enjoying the product of such creativity. On the illegitimacy of such patent restriction, see Rothbard, *Man, Economy and State*, pp. 652-660. (See also, Chapter 10, Section 7: Patents and Copyrights.)

[11]Kolko, *Triumph*, pp. 30-39.

on the relation of the state to business. Primarily an organization of big businessmen, it pushed for the tactical and theoretical alliance of business and government, a primitive version of the modern business-government partnership. Contrary to the consensus of many conservatives, it was not ideological innocence that led them to create a statist economic order — they knew what they were doing and constantly said so.

The working partnership of business and government was the result of the conscious activities of organizations such as the NCF created in 1900 (coincided with the birth of what is called the "Progressive Movement") to fight with increasing and sustained vigor against what it considered to be its twin enemies: "the socialists and radicals among workers and middle class reformers, and the 'anarchists' among the businessmen" (as the NCF characterized the National Association of Manufacturers). The smaller businessmen, who constituted the NAM, formed an opposition to the new liberalism that developed through cooperation between political leaders such as Theodore Roosevelt, William H. Taft and Woodrow Wilson, and the financial and corporate leaders in the NCF and other similar organizations. The NCF before World War I was "the most important single organization of the socially conscious big businessmen and their academic and political theorists." The NCF "took the lead in educating the businessmen to the changing needs in political economy which accompanied the changing nature of America's business system."[12]

The early leaders of the NCF were such big business leaders as Marcus A. Hanna, utilities magnate Samuel B.

[12]Weinstein, *The Corporate Ideal*, p. 82.

Insull, Chicago banker Franklin MacVeagh (later Secretary of the treasury), Charles Francis Adams and several partners in J. P. Morgan & Co. The largest contributor to the group was Andrew Carnegie; other important members of the executive committee included George W. Perkins, Elbert H. Gary (a Morgan associate and a head of U. S. Steel after Carnegie), Cyrus McCormick, Theodore N. Vail (president of AT&T) and George Cortelyou (head of Consolidated Gas).

The NCF sponsored legislation to promote the formation of "public utilities," a special privilege monopoly granted by the state, reserving an area of production to one company. Issuing a report on "Public Ownership of Public Utilities," the NCF established a general framework for regulatory laws, stating that utilities should be conducted by legalized independent commissions. Of such regulation one businessman wrote another: "Twenty-five years ago we would have regarded it as a species of socialism"; but seeing that the railroads were both submitting to and apparently profiting from regulation, the NCF's self-appointed job of "educating" municipal utilities corporations became much easier.

Regulation in general, far from coming against the wishes of the regulated interests, was openly welcomed by them in nearly every case. As Upton Sinclair said of the meat industry, which he is given credit for having tamed, "the federal inspection of meat was historically established at the packers' request. . . . It is maintained and paid for by the people of the United States for the benefit of the packers."[13]

However, one interesting fact comes in here to refute the Marxist theory further. For the Marxists hold that there are fundamentally two opposing "interests" which clash in

[13]Kolko, *Triumph*, p. 103.

history: the capitalists and the workers. But what we have seen, essentially, is that the interests (using the word in a journalistic sense) of neither the capitalists nor the workers, so-called, were uniform or clear-cut. The interests of the larger capitalists seemed to coincide, as they saw it, and were clearly opposed to the interests of the smaller capitalists. (However, there were conflicts among the big capitalists, such as between the Morgan and Rockefeller interests during the 1900s, as illustrated in the regimes of Roosevelt and Taft.) The larger capitalists saw regulation as being in their interest, and competition as opposed to it; with the smaller businessmen, the situation was reversed. The workers for the larger businesses also may have temporarily gained at the expense of others through slight wage increases caused by restrictions on production. (The situation is made even more complicated when we remember that the Marxist belief is that one's relationship to the means of production determines one's interests and hence, apparently, one's ideas. Yet people with basically the same relationship often had different "interests" and ideas. If this in turn is explained by a Marxist in terms of "mystification," an illuminating explanation in a libertarian context, then mystification itself is left to be explained. For if one's ideas and interests are an automatic function of the economic system and one's relationship to the means of production, how can "mystification" arise at all?) In any case, congressional hearings during the administration of Theodore Roosevelt revealed that "the big Chicago packers wanted more meat inspection both to bring the small packers under control and to aid them in their position in the export trade." Formally representing the large Chicago packers, Thomas E. Wilson publicly announced: "We are now and have always been in favor of the extension of the inspection."[14]

In both word and deed American businessmen sought to replace the last remnants of laissez-faire in the United States with government regulation – for their own benefit. Speaking at Columbia University in February 1908, George W. Perkins, a Morgan associate, said that the corporation "must welcome federal supervision administered by practical businessmen."[15]

As early as 1908, Andrew Carnegie and Ingalls had suggested to the NCF that it push for an American version of the British Board of Trade, which would have the power to judge mergers and other industrial actions. As Carnegie put it, this had "been found sufficient in other countries and will be so with us. We must have our industrial as we have a Judicial Supreme Court."[16] Carnegie also endorsed government actions to end ruinous competition.

> It always comes back to me that government control, and that alone, will properly solve the problem. ... There is nothing alarming in this; capital is perfectly safe in the gas company, although it is under court control. So will all capital be, although under government control.[17]

AT&T, controlled by J. P. Morgan as of 1907, also sought regulation. The company got what it wanted in 1910, when telephones were placed under the jurisdiction of the ICC, and

[14]Kolko, *Triumph*, p. 103.
[15]Kolko, *Triumph*, p. 129.
[16]Weinstein, *The Corporate Ideal*, p. 180.
[17]Kolko, *Triumph*, p. 180.

rate wars became a thing of the past. President T. N. Vail of AT&T said, "we believe in and were the first to advocate ... governmental control and regulation of public utilities."

By June of 1911, Elbert H. Gary of U. S. Steel appeared before a congressional committee and announced to astonished members, "I believe we must come to enforced publicity and governmental control even as to prices." He virtually offered to turn price control over to the government. Kolko states that,

> the reason Gary and Carnegie were offering the powers of price control to the federal government was not known to the congressmen, who were quite unaware of the existing price anarchy in steel. The proposals of Gary and Carnegie, the Democratic majority on the committee reported, were really "semisocialistic" and hardly worth endorsing.[18]

Gary also proposed that a commission similar to the ICC be set up to grant, suspend and revoke licenses for trade and to regulate prices.

In the fall of 1911, the NCF moved in two fronts: it sent a questionnaire to 30,000 businessmen to seek out their positions on a number of issues. Businessmen favored regulation of trade by three to one.

In November of 1911, Theodore Roosevelt proposed a national commission to control organization and capitalization of all inter-state businesses. The proposal won an immediate and enthusiastic response from Wall Street.

In 1912, Arthur Eddy, an eminent corporation lawyer, working much of the time with Standard Oil, and one of

[18]Kolko, *Triumph*, pp. 173-174.

the architects of the FTC, stated boldly in his magnum opus, The New Competition, what had been implicit in the doctrines of businessmen all along: Eddy trumpeted that "competition was inhuman and war, and that war was hell." Thus did big businessmen believe and act.

Meanwhile, back at the bank, J. P. Morgan was not to be left out. For Morgan, because of his ownership or control of many major corporations, was in the fight for regulation from the earliest days onward. Morgan's financial power and reputation were largely the result of his operations with the American and European governments; his many dealings in currency manipulations and loans to oppressive European states earned him the reputation of a "rescuer of governments." One crucial aspect of the banking system at the beginning of the 1900s was the relative decrease in New York's financial dominance and the rise of competitors. Morgan was fully aware of the diffusion of banking power that was taking place, and it disturbed him.

Hence, bankers too turned to regulation. From very early days, Morgan had championed the cause of a central bank, of gaining control over the nation's credit through a board of leading bankers under government supervision. By 1907, the NCF had taken up the call for a more elastic currency and for greater centralization of banking.

Nelson Aldrich proposed a reform bank act and called a conference of twenty-two bankers from twelve cities to discuss it. The purpose of the conference was to "discuss winning the banking community over to government control directed by the bankers for their own ends." A leading banker, Paul Warburg, stated that "it would be a blessing to get these small banks out of the way."[19]

Most of his associates agreed. In 1913, two years after the conference, and after any squabbles over specifics, the Federal Reserve Act was passed. The big bankers were pleased.

These were not the only areas in which businessmen and their political henchmen were active. Indeed, ideologically speaking, they were behind innumerable "progressive" actions, and even financed such magazines as The New Republic. Teddy Roosevelt made a passing reference to the desirability of an income tax in his 1906 message to Congress, and the principle received support from such businessmen as George W. Perkins and Carnegie, who often referred to the unequal distribution of wealth as "one of the crying evils of our day." Many businessmen opposed it, but the Wall Street Journal said that it was certainly in favor of it.

The passage of the Clayton Antitrust Act and the creation of the Federal Trade Commission occurred in 1914. Once established, the FTC began its attempt to secure the "confidence" of "well-intentioned" businessmen. In a speech before the NCF, one of the pro-regulation powerhouses, J. W. Jenks, "affirmed the general feeling of relief among the leaders of large corporations and their understanding that the FTC was helpful to the corporations in every way."[20]

In this crucially important era, I have focused on one point: big business was a major source of American statism. Further researches would show, I am convinced, that big business and financial leaders were also the dominant force behind America's increasingly interventionist foreign policy,

[19]Kolko, *Triumph*, p. 183.

[20]Weinstein, *The Corporate Ideal*, p. 91.

and behind the ideology of modern liberalism. In fact, by this analysis sustained research might show American liberal intellectuals to be the "running dogs" of big businessmen, to twist a Marxist phrase a bit.

Consider the fact that the New Republic has virtually always taken the role of defender of the corporate state which big businessmen carefully constructed over decades. Consider the fact that such businessmen as Carnegie not only supported all the groups mentioned and the programs referred to, but also supported such things as the Big Navy movement at the turn of the century. He sold steel to the United States government that went into the building of the ships and he saw in the Venezuela boundary dispute the possibility of a large order for armor from the United States Navy.[21] Carnegie, along with Rockefeller and, later, Ford, was responsible for sustained support of American liberalism through the foundations set up in his name.

J. P. Morgan, the key financial leader, was also a prime mover of American statism. His foreign financial dealings led him to become deeply involved with Britain during World War I, and this involvement in turn led him to help persuade Wilson to enter the war on Britain's behalf, to help save billions of dollars of loans which would be lost in the event of a German victory.

In a more interesting light, consider the statements made in 1914 by S. Thruston Ballard, owner of the largest wheat

[21]Walter LeFeber, *The New Empire: An Interpretation of American Expansion, 1860-1890* (Ithaca: Cornell University press, 1963), pp. 239, 273n. The note on Carnegie's linking of the Venezuela boundary dispute with obtaining large orders of steel from the Navy was taken from Carnegie's correspondence.

refinery in the world. Ballard not only supported vocational schools as a part of the public schools (which would transfer training costs to taxpayers), restrictions on immigration, and a national minimum wage, he saw and proposed a way to "cure" unemployment. He advocated a federal employment service, public works, and if these wee insufficient, "government concentration camps where work with a small wage would be provided, supplemented by agricultural and industrial training."[22] Consider the role of big businessmen in pushing through public education in many states after World War I. Senator Wadsworth spoke before a NCF group in 1916, pointing out that compulsory government education was needed "to protect the nation against destruction from within. It is to train the boy and girl to be good citizens, to protect against ignorance and dissipation." This meant that the reason to force children to go to school, at gunpoint if necessary, was so that they could be brainwashed into accepting the status quo, almost explicitly so that their capacity for dissent (i.e., their capacity for independent thinking) could be destroyed. Thus did Wadsworth also advocate compulsory and universal military training: "Our people shall be prepared mentally as well as in a purely military sense. We must let our young men know that they owe some responsibility to this country."

Indeed, we find V. E. Macy, president of the NCF at the close of the war, stating that it was not "beside the mark to call attention to the nearly thirty million minors marching steadily toward full citizenship," and ask "at what stage of their journey we should lend assistance to the work of quickening … the sense of responsibility and partnership in the

[22]Weinstein, *The Corporate Ideal*, p. 91.

business of maintaining and perfecting the splendid social, industrial, and commercial structure which has been reared under the American flag." The need, Macy noted, was most urgent. Among American youths there was a widespread "indifference toward, and aloofness from, individual responsibility for the successful maintenance and upbuilding of the industrial and commercial structure which is the indispensable shelter of us all."[23]

Big business, then, was behind the existence and curriculum of the public educational system, explicitly to teach young minds to submit and obey, to pay homage to the "corporate liberal" system which the politicians, a multitude of intellectuals and many big businessmen created.

My intention here simply has been to present an alternative model of historical interpretation of key events in this one crucial era of American history, an interpretation which is neither Marxist, liberal nor conservative, but which may have some elements in common with each.

From a more ideological perspective, my purpose has been to present an accurate portrait of on aspect of "how we got here," and indicate a new way of looking at the present system in America.

To a large degree it has been and remains big businessmen who are the fountainheads of American statism. If libertarians are seeking allies in their struggle for liberty, then I suggest that they look elsewhere. Conservatives, too, should benefit from this presentation, and begin to see big business as a destroyer, not as a unit, of the free market. Liberals should also benefit, and reexamine their own premises about the market and regulation. Specifically, they might

[23]Weinstein, *The Corporate Ideal*, pp. 133-135.

reconsider the nature of a freemarket, and ponder on the question of why big business has been opposed to precisely that. Isn't it odd that the interests of liberals and key big businessmen have always coincided? The Marxists, too, might rethink their economics, and reconsider whether or not capitalism leads to monopoly. Since it can be shown scientifically that economic calculation is impossible in a purely socialistic economy, and that pure statism is not good for man, perhaps the Marxists might also look at the real nature of a complete free market, undiluted by state control.

Libertarians themselves should take heart. Our hope lies, as strange as it may seem, not with any remnants from an illusory "golden age" of individualism, which never existed, but with tomorrow. Our day has not come and gone. It has never existed at all. It is our task to see that it will exist in the future. The choice and the battle are ours.

CHAPTER

THREE

THE IRON FIST BEHIND THE INVISIBLE HAND

KEVIN CARSON

Introduction

Manorialism, commonly, is recognized to have been founded by robbery and usurpation; a ruling class established itself by force, and then compelled the peasantry to work for the profit of their lords. But no system of exploitation,including capitalism, has ever been created by the action of a free market. Capitalism was founded on an act of robbery as massive as feudalism. It has been sustained to the present by continual state intervention to protect its system of privilege, without which its survival is unimaginable.

The current structure of capital ownership and organization of production in our so-called "market" economy, reflects

https://c4ss.org/content/24158

coercive state intervention prior to and extraneous to the market. From the outset of the industrial revolution, what is nostalgically called "laissez-faire" was in fact a system of continuing state intervention to subsidize accumulation, guarantee privilege, and maintain work discipline.

Most such intervention is tacitly assumed by mainstream right-libertarians as part of a "market" system. Although a few intellectually honest ones like Rothbard and Hess were willing to look into the role of coercion in creating capitalism, the Chicago school and Randroids take existing property relations and class power as a given. Their ideal "free market" is merely the current system minus the progressive regulatory and welfare state — i.e., nineteenth century robber baron capitalism.

But genuine markets have a value for the libertarian left, and we shouldn't concede the term to our enemies. In fact, capitalism — a system of power in which ownership and control are divorced from labor — could not survive in a free market. As a mutualist anarchist, I believe that expropriation of surplus value — i.e., capitalism — cannot occur without state coercion to maintain the privilege of usurer, landlord, and capitalist. It was for this reason that the free market anarchist Benjamin Tucker — from whom right-libertarians selectively borrow — regarded himself as a libertarian socialist. It is beyond my ability or purpose here to describe a world where a true market system could have developed without such state intervention. A world in which peasants had held onto their land and property was widely distributed, capital was freely available to laborers through mutual banks, productive technology was freely available in every country without patents, and every people was free to develop locally without colonial robbery, is beyond our imagination. But it would have been a world of decentralized, small-scale production for local use, owned and controlled by those who did the work — as different from our world as day from night, or freedom from slavery.

The Subsidy of History

Accordingly, the single biggest subsidy to modern corporate capitalism is the subsidy of history, by which capital was originally accumulated in a few hands, and labor was deprived of access to the means of production and forced to sell itself on the buyer's terms. The current system of concentrated capital ownership and large-scale corporate organization is the direct beneficiary of that original structure of power and property ownership, which has perpetuated itself over the centuries.

For capitalism as we know it to come about, it was essential first of all for labor to be separated from property. Marxians and other radical economists commonly refer to the process as "primitive accumulation." "What the capitalist system demanded was... a degraded and almost servile condition of the mass of the people, the transformation of them into mercenaries, and of their means of labor into capital." That meant expropriating the land, "to which the [peasantry] has the same feudal rights as the lord himself."[1]

To grasp the enormity of the process, we must understand that the nobility's rights in land under the manorial economy were entirely a feudal legal fiction deriving from conquest.

[1]Marx, "Chapter 27: The Expropriation," *Capital* vol. 1.

The peasants who cultivated the land of England in 1650 were descendants of those who had occupied it since time immemorial. By any standard of morality, it was their property in every sense of the word. The armies of William the Conqueror, by no right other than force, had compelled these peasant proprietors to pay rent on their own land.

J. L. and Barbara Hammond treated the sixteenth century village and open field system as a survival of the free peasant society of Anglo-Saxon times, with landlordism superimposed on it. The gentry saw surviving peasant rights as a hindrance to progress and efficient farming; a revolution in their own power was a way of breaking peasant resistance. Hence the agricultural community was "taken to pieces ... and reconstructed in the manner in which a dictator reconstructs a free government."[2]

When the Tudors gave expropriated monastic lands to the nobility, the latter "drove out, en masse, the hereditary sub tenants and threw their holdings into one."[3] This stolen land, about a fifth of the arable land of England, was the first large-scale expropriation of the peasantry.

Another major theft of peasant land was the "reform" of land law by the seventeenth century Restoration Parliament. The aristocracy abolished feudal tenures and converted their own estate in the land, until then "only a feudal title," into "rights of modern private property." In the process, they abolished the tenure rights of copyholders. Copyholders were de jure tenants under feudal law, but once they paid a negligible quit-rent fixed by custom, the land was theirs to sell or bequeath. In substance copyhold tenure was a

[2] *The Village Labourer* 27-28, 35-36.

[3] Marx, "The Expropriation..."

manorial equivalent of freehold; but since it derived from custom it was enforceable only in the manor courts. Under the "reform," tenants in copyhold became tenants at-will, who could be evicted or charged whatever rent their lord saw fit.[4]

Another form of expropriation, which began in late medieval times and increased drastically in the eighteenth century, was the enclosure of commons–in which, again, the peasants communally had as absolute a right of property as any defended by today's "property rights" advocates. Not counting enclosures before 1700, the Hammonds estimated total enclosures in the eighteenth and nineteenth centuries at a sixth or a fifth of the arable land in England.[5] E. J. Hobsbawm and George Rude estimated enclosures between 1750 and 1850 alone as transforming "something like one quarter of the cultivated acreage from open field, common land, meadow or waste into private fields. . . ."[6]

The ruling classes saw the peasants' right in commons as a source of economic independence from capitalist and landlord, and thus a threat to be destroyed. Enclosure eliminated "a dangerous centre of indiscipline" and compelled workers to sell their labor on the masters' terms. Arthur Young, a Lincolnshire gentleman, described the commons as "a breeding-ground for 'barbarians,' 'nursing up a mischievous race of people'." "[E]very one but an idiot knows," he wrote, "that the lower classes must be kept poor, or they will never be industrious." The Commercial and Agricultural Magazine warned in 1800 that leaving the laborer "possessed of more

---

[4]Marx, "The Expropriation..."

[5]*Village Labourer* 42.

[6]*Captain Swing* 27.

land than his family can cultivate in the evenings" meant that "the farmer can no longer depend on him for constant work."[7] Sir Richard Price commented on the conversion of self-sufficient proprietors into "a body of men who earn their subsistence by working for others." There would, "perhaps, be more labour, because there will be more compulsion to it."[8]

Marx cited parliamentary "acts of enclosure" as evidence that the commons, far from being the "private property of the great landlords who have taken the place of the feudal lords," actually required "a parliamentary coup detat... for its transformation into private property."[9] The process of primitive accumulation, in all its brutality, was summed up by the same author:

> These new freedmen [i.e. former serfs] became sellers of themselves only after they had been robbed of all their own means of production, and of all the guarantees of existence afforded by the old feudal arrangements. And the history of this, their expropriation, is written in the annals of mankind in letters of blood and fire.[10]

Even then, the working class was not sufficiently powerless. The state had to regulate the movement of labor, serve as a labor exchange on behalf of capitalists, and maintain order. The system of parish regulation of the movement of

[7]Thompson, *The Making of the English Working Class* 219-220, 358.
[8]Marx, "The Expropriation..."
[9]"The Expropriation..."
[10]"Chapter 26: The Secret of Primitive Accumulation," *Capital* Vol. 1.

people, under the poor laws and vagrancy laws, resembled the internal passport system of South Africa, or the reconstruction era Black Codes. It "had the same effect on the English agricultural labourer," Marx wrote, "as the edict of the Tartar Boris Godunov on the Russian peasantry."[11] Adam Smith ventured that there was "scarce a poor man in England of forty years of age... who has not in some part of his life felt himself most cruelly oppressed by this ill-contrived law of settlements."[12]

The state maintained work discipline by keeping laborers from voting with their feet. It was hard to persuade parish authorities to grant a man a certificate entitling him to move to another parish to seek work. Workers were forced to stay put and bargain for work in a buyer's market.[13]

At first glance this would seem to be inconvenient for parishes with a labor shortage.[14] Factories were built at sources of water power, generally removed from centers of population. Thousands of workers were needed to be imported from far away. But the state saved the day by setting itself up as a middleman in providing labor-poor parishes with cheap surplus labor from elsewhere, depriving workers of the ability to bargain for better terms. A considerable trade arose in child laborers who were in no position to bargain in any case.[15]

Relief "was seldom bestowed without the parish claiming the exclusive right of disposing, at their pleasure, of all

[11]"The Expropriation..."

[12]*Wealth of Nations* 61.

[13]Smith 60-61.

[14]Smith 60.

[15]The Hammonds, *The Town Labourer* 1:146.

the children of the person receiving relief," in the words of the Committee on Parish Apprentices, 1815.[16] Even when Poor Law commissioners encouraged migration to labor-poor parishes, they discouraged adult men and "Preference was given to 'widows with large families of children or handicraftsmen... with large families.'" In addition, the availability of cheap labor from the poor-law commissioners was deliberately used to drive down wages; farmers would discharge their own day-laborers and instead apply to the overseer for help.[17]

Although the Combination Laws theoretically applied to masters as well as workmen, in practice they were not enforced against the latter.[18] "A Journeyman Cotton Spinner" — a pamphleteer quoted by E. P. Thompson[19] — described "an abominable combination existing amongst the masters," in which workers who had left their masters because of disagreement over wages were effectively black-listed. The Combination Laws required suspects to answer interrogations on oath, empowered magistrates to give summary judgment, and allowed summary forfeiture of funds accumulated to aid the families of strikers.[20] And the laws setting maximum rates of pay amounted to a state enforced system of combination for the masters. As Adam Smith put it, "[w]henever the legislature attempts to regulate the differences between the masters and their workmen, its counsellors are always

[16]The Hammonds, *The Town Labourer* 1:44, 147.
[17]Thompson 223-224.
[18]Smith 61; the Hammonds, *Town Labourer* 1:74.
[19]199-202.
[20]*Town Labourer* 123-127.

the masters."[21]

The working class lifestyle under the factory system, with its new forms of social control, was a radical break with the past. It involved drastic loss of control over their own work. The seventeenth century work calendar was still heavily influenced by medieval custom. Although there were long days in spurts between planting and harvest, intermittent periods of light work and the proliferation of saints days combined to reduce average work-time well below our own. And the pace of work was generally determined by the sun or the biological rhythms of the laborer, who got up after a decent night's sleep, and sat down to rest when he felt like it. The cottager who had access to common land, even when he wanted extra income from wage labor, could take work on a casual basis and then return to working for himself. This was an unacceptable degree of independence from a capitalist standpoint.

> In the modern world most people have to adapt themselves to some kind of discipline, and to observe other' people's timetables, ... or work under other people's orders, but we have to remember that the population that was flung into the brutal rhythm of the factory had earned its living in relative freedom, and that the discipline of the early factory was particularly savage.... No economist of the day, in estimating the gains or losses of factory employment, ever allowed for the strain and violence that a man suffered in his feelings when he passed from a life in which he could smoke or eat, or dig or sleep as he pleased, to one in which somebody turned the key

[21] 61.

> on him, and for fourteen hours he had not even the right to whistle. It was like entering the airless and laughterless life of a prison.[22]

The factory system could not have been imposed on workers without first depriving them of alternatives, and forcibly denying access to any source of economic independence. No unbroken human being, with a sense of freedom or dignity, would have submitted to factory discipline. Stephen Marglin compared the nineteenth century textile factory, staffed by pauper children bought at the workhouse slave market, to Roman brick and pottery factories which were manned by slaves. In Rome, factory production was exceptional in manufactures dominated by freemen. The factory system, throughout history, has been possible only with a work force deprived of any viable alternative.

> The surviving facts... strongly suggest that whether work was organized along factory lines was in Roman times determined, not by technological considerations, but by the relative power of the two producing classes. Freedmen and citizens had sufficient power to maintain a guild organization. Slaves had no power — and ended up in factories.[23]

The problem with the old "putting out" system, in which cottage workers produced textiles on a contractual basis, was that it only eliminated worker control of the product. The factory system, by eliminating worker control of the production process, had the advantage of discipline and supervision, with workers organized under an overseer.

---

[22]The Hammonds, *Town Labourer* 1:33-34.

[23]"What Do Bosses Do?"

> The origin and success of the factory lay not in technological superiority, but in the substitution of the capitalist's for the worker's control of the work process and the quantity of output, in the change in the workman's choice from one of how much to work and produce, based on his preferences for leisure and goods, to one of whether or not to work at all, which of course is hardly much of a choice.

Marglin took Adam Smith's classic example of the division of labor in pin-making, and stood it on its head. The increased efficiency resulted, not from the division of labor as such, but from dividing and sequencing the process into separate tasks in order to reduce set-up time. This could have been accomplished by a single cottage workman separating the various tasks and then performing them sequentially (i.e., drawing out the wire for an entire run of production, then straightening it, then cutting it, etc.).

> Without specialization, the capitalist had no essential role to play in the production process. If each producer could himself integrate the component tasks of pin manufacture into a marketable product, he would soon discover that he had no need to deal with the market for pins through the intermediation of the putter-outer. He could sell directly and appropriate to himself the profit that the capitalist derived from mediating between the producer and the market.

This principle is at the center of the history of industrial technology for the last two hundred years. Even given the necessity of factories for some forms of large-scale, capital-intensive manufacturing, there is usually a choice between alternate productive technologies within the factory. Industry has consistently chosen technologies which de-skill workers and shift decision-making upward into the managerial hierarchy. As long ago as 1835, Dr. Andrew Ure (the ideological grandfather of Taylorism and Fordism), argued that the more skilled the workman, "the more self-willed and... the less fit a component of a mechanical system" he became. The solution was to eliminate processes which required "peculiar dexterity and steadiness of hand... from the cunning workman" and replace them by a "mechanism, so self-regulating, that a child may superintend it."[24] And the principle has been followed throughout the twentieth century. William Lazonick, David Montgomery, David Noble, and Katherine Stone have produced an excellent body of work on this theme. Even though corporate experiments in worker self-management increase morale and productivity, and reduce injuries and absenteeism, beyond the hopes of management, they are usually abandoned out of fear of loss of control.

Christopher Lasch, in his foreword to Noble's America by Design, characterized the process of de-skilling in this way:

> The capitalist, having expropriated the worker's property, gradually expropriated his technical knowledge as well, asserting his own mastery over production.... The expropriation of the worker's technical knowledge had as a logical consequence the growth of modern management, in which technical knowledge came to be concentrated. As the scientific management movement split up production into its

[24] *Philosophy of Manufactures*, in Thompson 360.

> component procedures, reducing the worker to an appendage of the machine, a great expansion of technical and supervisory personnel took place in order to oversee the productive process as a whole.[25]

The expropriation of the peasantry and imposition of the factory labor system was not accomplished without resistance; the workers knew exactly what was being done to them and what they had lost. During the 1790s, when rhetoric from the Jacobins and Tom Paine were widespread among the radicalized working class, the rulers of "the cradle of liberty" lived in terror that the country would be swept by revolution. The system of police state controls over the population resembled an alien occupation regime. The Hammonds referred to correspondence between north-country magistrates and the Home Office, in which the law was frankly treated "as an instrument not of justice but of repression," and the working classes "appear[ed]... conspicuously as a helot population."[26]

> ... in the light of the Home Office papers, ... none of the personal rights attaching to Englishmen possessed any reality for the working classes. The magistrates and their clerks recognized no limit to their powers over the freedom and the movements of working men. The Vagrancy Laws seemed to supercede the entire charter of an Englishman's liberties. They were used to put into prison any man or woman of the working class who seemed to the magistrate an inconvenient or disturbing character. They offered

[25] xi-xii.

[26] *Town Labourer* 72.

> the easiest and most expeditious way of proceeding against any one who tried to collect money for the families of locked-out workmen, or to disseminate literature that the magistrates thought undesirable.[27]

Peel's "bobbies" — professional law enforcement — replaced the posse comitatus system because the latter was inadequate to control a population of increasingly disaffected workmen. In the time of the Luddite and other disturbances, crown officials warned that "to apply the Watch and Ward Act would be to put arms into the hands of the most powerfully disaffected." At the outset of the wars with France, Pitt ended the practice of quartering the army in alehouses, mixed with the general population. Instead, the manufacturing districts were covered with barracks, as "purely a matter of police." The manufacturing areas "came to resemble a country under military occupation."[28]

Pitt's police state was supplemented by quasi-private vigilantism, in the time-honored tradition of blackshirts and death squads ever since. For example the "Association for the Protection of Property against Republicans and Levellers" — an anti-Jacobin association of gentry and mill-owners — conducted house-to-house searches and organized Guy Fawkes-style effigy burnings against Paine; "Church and King" mobs terrorised suspected radicals[29]

Thompson characterized this system of control as "political and social apartheid," and argued that "the revolution which did not happen in England was fully as devastating"

[27] *Ibid.* 80.

[28] *Ibid.* 91-92.

[29] Chapter Five, "Planting the Liberty Tree," in Thompson.

as the one that did happen in France.[30]

Finally, the state aided the growth of manufactures through mercantilism. Modern exponents of the "free market" generally treat mercantilism as a "misguided" attempt to promote some unified national interest, adopted out of sincere ignorance of economic principles. In fact, the architects of mercantilism knew exactly what they were doing. Mercantilism was extremely efficient for its real purpose: making wealthy manufacturing interests rich at the expense of everyone else. Adam Smith consistently attacked mercantilism, not as a product of economic error, but as a quite intelligent attempt by powerful interests to enrich themselves through the coercive power of the state.

British manufacturing was created by state intervention to shut out foreign goods, give British shipping a monopoly of foreign commerce, and stamp out foreign competition by force. As an example of the latter, British authorities in India destroyed the Bengalese textile industry, makers of the highest quality fabric in the world. Although they had not adopted steam-driven methods of production, there is a real possibility that they would have done so, had India remained politically and economically independent. The once prosperous territory of Bengal is today occupied by Bangladesh and the Calcutta area.[31]

The American, German and Japanese industrial systems were created by the same mercantilist policies, with massive tariffs on industrial goods. "Free trade" was adopted by safely established industrial powers, who used "laissez-faire" as an ideological weapon to prevent potential rivals from

[30] 197-198.

[31] Chomsky, *World Orders Old and New.*

following the same path of industrialization. Capitalism has never been established by means of the free market, or even by the primary action of the bourgeoisie. It has always been established by a revolution from above, imposed by a pre-capitalist ruling class. In England, it was the landed aristocracy; in France, Napoleon II's bureaucracy; in Germany, the Junkers; in Japan, the Meiji. In America, the closest approach to a "natural" bourgeois evolution, industrialization was carried out by a mercantilist aristocracy of Federalist shipping magnates and landlords,[32]

Romantic medievalists like Chesterton and Belloc described the process in the high middle ages by which serfdom had gradually withered away, and the peasants had transformed themselves into de facto freeholders who paid a nominal quit-rent. The feudal class system was disintegrating and being replaced by a much more libertarian and less exploitative one. Immanuel Wallerstein argued that the likely outcome would have been "a system of relatively equal small-scale producers, further flattening out the aristocracies and decentralizing the political structures." By 1650 the trend had been reversed, and there was "a reasonably high level of continuity between the families that had been high strata" in 1450 and 1650. Capitalism, far from being "the overthrow of a backward aristocracy by a progressive bourgeoisie," "was brought into existence by a landed aristocracy which transformed itself into a bourgeoisie because the old system was disintegrating."[33] This is echoed in part by Arno Mayer,[34] who argued for continuity between the

[32]Harrington, *Twilight of Capitalism.*

[33]*Historical Capitalism* 41-42, 105-106.

[34]*The Persistence of the Old Regime.*

landed aristocracy and the capitalist ruling class.

The process by which the high medieval civilization of peasant proprietors, craft guilds and free cities was overthrown, was vividly described by Kropotkin.[35] Before the invention of gunpowder, the free cities repelled royal armies more often than not, and won their independence from feudal dues. And these cities often made common cause with peasants in their struggles to control the land. The absolutist state and the capitalist revolution it imposed became possible only when artillery could reduce fortified cities with a high degree of efficiency, and the king could make war on his own people. And in the aftermath of this conquest, the Europe of William Morris was left devastated, depopulated, and miserable.

Peter Tosh had a song called "Four Hundred Years." Although the white working class has suffered nothing like the brutality of black slavery, there has nevertheless been a "four hundred years" of oppression for all of us under the system of state capitalism established in the seventeenth century. Ever since the birth of the first states six thousand years ago, political coercion has allowed one ruling class or another to live off other people's labor. But since the seventeenth century the system of power has become increasingly conscious, unified, and global in scale. The current system of transnational state capitalism, without rival since the collapse of the soviet bureaucratic class system, is a direct outgrowth of the seizure of power "four hundred years" ago. Orwell had it backwards. The past is a "boot smashing a human face." Whether the future is more of the same depends on what we do now.

[35] *Mutual Aid* 225.

Ideological Hegemony

Ideological hegemony is the process by which the exploited come to view the world through a conceptual framework provided to them by their exploiters. It acts first of all to conceal class conflict and exploitation behind a smokescreen of "national unity" or "general welfare." Those who point to the role of the state as guarantor of class privilege are denounced, in theatrical tones of moral outrage, for "class warfare." If anyone is so unpardonably "extremist" as to describe the massive foundation of state intervention and subsidy upon which corporate capitalism rests, he is sure to be rebuked for "Marxist class war rhetoric" (Bob Novak), or "robber baron rhetoric" (Treasury Secretary O'Neill).

The ideological framework of "national unity" is taken to the point that "this country," "society," or "our system of government" is set up as an object of gratitude for "the freedoms we enjoy." Only the most unpatriotic notice that our liberties, far from being granted to us by a generous and benevolent government, were won by past resistance against the state. Charters and bills of rights were not grants from the state, but were forced on the state from below.

If our liberties belong to us by right of birth, as a moral fact of nature, it follows that we owe the state no debt of gratitude for not violating them, any more than we owe our thanks to another individual for refraining from robbing or killing us. Simple logic implies that, rather than being grateful to "the freest country on earth," we should raise hell every time it infringes on our liberty. After all, that's how we got our liberty in the first place. When another individual puts his hand in our pocket to enrich himself at our expense, our natural instinct is to resist. But thanks to patriotism, the ruling class is able to transform their hand in our pocket into "society" or "our country."

The religion of national unity is most pathological in regard to "defense" and foreign policy. The manufacture of foreign crisis and war hysteria has been used since the beginning of history to suppress threats to class rule. The crooked politicians may work for the "special interests" domestically, but when those same politicians engineer a war it is a matter of loyalty to "our country."

The Chairman of the JCS, in discussing the "defense" posture, will refer with a straight face to "national security threats" faced by the U. S., and describe the armed forces of some official enemy like China as far beyond "legitimate defensive requirements." The quickest way to put oneself beyond the pale is to point out that all these "threats" involve what some country on the other side of the world is doing within a hundred miles of its own border. Another offense against fatherland worship is to judge the actions of the United States, in its global operations to keep the Third World safe for ITT and United Fruit Company, by the same standard of "legitimate defensive requirements" applied to China.

In the official ideology, America's wars by definition are always fought "for our liberties," to "defend our country," or in the smarmy world of Maudlin Albright, a selfless desire to promote "peace and freedom" in the world. To suggest that the real defenders of our liberties took up arms against the government, or that the national security state is a greater threat to our liberties than any foreign enemy we have ever faced, is unforgivable. Above all, good Americans don't notice all those military advisers teaching death squads how to hack off the faces of union organizers and leave them in ditches, or to properly use pliers on a dissident's testicles. War crimes are only committed by defeated powers. (But as the Nazis learned in 1945, unemployed war criminals can usually find work with the new hegemonic power.)

After a century and a half of patriotic indoctrination by the statist education system, Americans have thoroughly internalized the "little red schoolhouse" version of American history. This authoritarian piety is so diametrically opposed to the beliefs of those who took up arms in the Revolution that the citizenry has largely forgotten what it means to be American. In fact, the authentic principles of Americanism have been stood on their head. Two hundred years ago, standing armies were feared as a threat to liberty and a breeding ground for authoritarian personalities; conscription was associated with the tyranny of Cromwell; wage labor was thought to be inconsistent with the independent spirit of a free citizen. Today, two hundred years later, Americans have been so Prussianized by sixty years of a garrison state and "wars" against one internal enemy or another, that they are conditioned to genuflect at the sight of a uniform. Draft dodgers are equivalent to child molesters. Most people work for some centralized corporate or state bureaucracy, where as a matter of course they are expected to obey orders from superiors, work under constant surveillance, and even piss in a cup on command.

During wartime, it becomes unpatriotic to criticize or question the government and dissent is identified with disloyalty. Absolute faith and obedience to authority is a litmus test of "Americanism." Foreign war is a very useful tool for manipulating the popular mind and keeping the domestic population under control. War is the easiest way to shift vast, unaccountable new powers to the State. People are most uncritically obedient at the very time they need to be most vigilant.

The greatest irony is that, in a country founded by revolution, "Americanism" is defined as respecting authority and resisting "subversion." The Revolution was a revolution indeed, in which the domestic political institutions of the colonies were forcibly overthrown. It was, in many times and places, a civil war between classes. But as Voltairine de Cleyre wrote a century ago in "Anarchism and American Traditions," the version in the history books is a patriotic conflict between our "Founding Fathers" and a foreign enemy. Those who can still quote Jefferson on the right of revolution are relegated to the "extremist" fringe, to be rounded up in the next war hysteria or red scare.

This ideological construct of a unified "national interest" includes the fiction of a "neutral" set of laws, which conceals the exploitative nature of the system of power we live under. Under corporate capitalism the relationships of exploitation are mediated by the political system to an extent unknown under previous class systems. Under chattel slavery and feudalism, exploitation was concrete and personalized in the producer's relationship with his master. The slave and peasant knew exactly who was screwing them. The modern worker, on the other hand, feels a painful pounding sensation, but has only a vague idea where it is coming from.

Besides its function of masking the ruling class interests behind a facade of "general welfare," ideological hegemony also manufactures divisions between the ruled. Through campaigns against "welfare cheats" and "deadbeats," and demands to "get tough on crime," the ruling class is able to channel the hostility of the middle and working classes against the underclass.

Especially nauseating is the phenomenon of "billionaire populism." Calls for bankruptcy and welfare "reform," and for wars on crime, are dressed up in pseudo-populist rhetoric, identifying the underclass as the chief parasites who feed off the producers' labor. In their "aw, shucks" symbolic universe, you'd think America was a *Readers Digest*/Norman Rockwell world with nothing but hard-working small businessmen and family farmers, on the one hand, and welfare cheats, deadbeats, union bosses and bureaucrats on the other. From listening to them, you'd never suspect that multi-billionaires or global corporations even exist, let alone that they might stand to benefit from such "populism."

In the real world, corporations are the biggest clients of the welfare state, the biggest bankruptcies are corporate chapter eleven filings, and the worst crimes are committed in corporate suites rather than on the streets. The real robbery of the average producer consists of profit and usury, extorted only with the help of the state — the real "big government" on our backs. But as long as the working class and the underclass are busy fighting each other, they won't notice who is really robbing them. As Stephen Biko said, "*The oppressors' most powerful weapon is the mind of the oppressed.*"

The Money Monopoly

In every system of class exploitation, a ruling class controls access to the means of production in order to extract tribute from labor. Under capitalism, access to capital is restricted by the money monopoly, by which the state or banking system is given a monopoly on the medium of exchange, and alternative media of exchange are prohibited. The money monopoly also includes entry barriers against cooperative banks and prohibitions against private issuance of banknotes, by which access to finance capital is restricted and interest rates are kept artificially high.

Just in passing, we might mention the monumental hypocrisy of the regulation of credit unions in the United States, which require that their membership must share some common bond, like working for the same employer. Imagine the outrage if IGA and Safeway lobbied for a national law to prohibit grocery co-ops unless the members all worked for the same company! One of the most notable supporters of these laws is Phil Gramm, that renowned "free marketeer" and economics professor — and foremost among the banking industry's whores in Congress.

Individualist and mutualist anarchists like William Greene,[36] Benjamin Tucker,[37] and J. B. Robertson,[38] viewed the money monopoly as central to the capitalist system of privilege. In a genuinely free banking market, any group of individuals could form a mutual bank and issue monetized credit in the form of bank notes against any form of collateral

[36] *Mutual Banking.*

[37] *Instead of a Book.*

[38] *The Economics of Liberty.*

they chose, with acceptance of these notes as tender being a condition of membership. Greene speculated that a mutual bank might choose to honor not only marketable property as collateral, but the "*pledging* ... [of] *future production*."[39] The result would be a reduction in interest rates, through competition, to the cost of administrative overhead — less than one percent.

Abundant cheap credit would drastically alter the balance of power between capital and labor, and returns on labor would replace returns on capital as the dominant form of economic activity. According to Robinson,

> Upon the monopoly rate of interest for money that is... forced upon us by law, is based the whole system of interest upon capital, that permeates all modern business.
>
> With free banking, interest upon bonds of all kinds and dividends upon stock would fall to the minimum bank interest charge. The so-called rent of houses... would fall to the cost of maintenance and replacement.
>
> All that part of the product which is now taken by interest would belong to the producer. Capital, however... defined, would practically cease to exist as an income producing fund, for the simple reason that if money, wherewith to buy capital, could be obtained for one-half of one per cent, capital itself could command no higher price.[40]

And the result would be a drastically improved bargaining position for tenants and workers against the owners of

[39] 73.
[40] 80-81.

land and capital. According to Gary Elkin, Tucker's free market anarchism carried certain inherent libertarian socialist implications:

> It's important to note that because of Tucker's proposal to increase the bargaining power of workers through access to mutual credit, his so-called Individualist anarchism is not only compatible with workers' control but would in fact promote it. For if access to mutual credit were to increase the bargaining power of workers to the extent that Tucker claimed it would, they would then be able to (1) demand and get workplace democracy, and (2) pool their credit buy and own companies collectively.

The banking monopoly was not only the "lynchpin of capitalism," but also the seed from which the landlord's monopoly grew. Without a money monopoly, the price of land would be much lower, and promote "the process of reducing rents toward zero."[41]

Given the worker's improved bargaining position, "capitalists' ability to extract surplus value from the labor of employees would be eliminated or at least greatly reduced."[42] As compensation for labor approached value-added, returns on capital were driven down by market competition, and the value of corporate stock consequently plummeted, the worker would become a de facto co-owner of his workplace, even if the company remained nominally stockholder-owned.

Near-zero interest rates would increase the independence of labor in all sorts of interesting ways. For one thing,

---

[41]Gary Elkin, "*Benjamin Tucker — Anarchist or Capitalist.*"
[42]Gary Elkin, *Mutual Banking*.

anyone with a twenty-year mortgage at 8% now could, in the absence of usury, pay it off in ten years. Most people in their 30s would have their houses paid off. Between this and the nonexistence of high-interest credit card debt, two of the greatest sources of anxiety to keep one's job at any cost would disappear. In addition, many workers would have large savings ("go to hell money"). Significant numbers would retire in their forties or fifties, cut back to part-time, or start businesses; with jobs competing for workers, the effect on bargaining power would be revolutionary.

Our hypothetical world of free credit in many ways resembles the situation in colonial societies. E. G. Wakefield, in *View of the Art of Colonization*, wrote of the unacceptably weak position of the employing class when self-employment with one's own property was readily available. In colonies, there was a tight labor market and poor labor discipline because of the abundance of cheap land. "Not only does the degree of exploitation of the wage-labourer remain indecently low. The wage-labourer loses into the bargain, along with the relation of dependence, also the sentiment of dependence on the abstemious capitalist."

> Where land is cheap and all men are free, where every one who so pleases can obtain a piece of land for himself, not only is labour very dear, as respects the labourers' share of the product, but the difficulty is to obtain combined labour at any price.

This environment also prevented the concentration of wealth, as Wakefield commented: "Few, even of those whose lives are unusually long, can accumulate great masses of wealth." As a result, colonial elites petitioned the mother country for imported labor and for restrictions on land for settlement. According to Wakefield's disciple Herman Merivale, there was an "urgent desire for cheaper and more subservient labourers — for a class to whom the capitalist might dictate terms, instead of being dictated to by them."[43]

In addition to all this, central banking systems perform additional service to the interests of capital. First of all, the chief requirement of finance capitalists is to avoid inflation, in order to allow predictable returns on investment. This is ostensibly the primary purpose of the Federal Reserve and other central banks. But at least as important is the role of the central banks in promoting what they consider a "natural" level of unemployment — until the 1990s around six per cent. The reason is that when unemployment goes much below this figure, labor becomes increasingly uppity and presses for better pay and working conditions and more autonomy. Workers are willing to take a lot less crap off the boss when they know they can find a job at least as good the next day. On the other hand, nothing is so effective in "getting your mind right" as the knowledge that people are lined up to take your job.

The Clinton "prosperity" is a seeming exception to this principle. As unemployment threatened to drop below the four per cent mark, some members of the Federal Reserve agitated to raise interest rates and take off the "inflationary" pressure by throwing a few million workers on the street. But as Greenspan[44] testified before the Senate Banking Committee, the situation was unique. Given the degree

[43]Maurice Dobb, *Studies in the Development of Capitalism*; Marx, Chapter 33: "*The New Theory of Colonialism*," in *Capital* Vol. 1.

[44]Testimony of Chairman Alan Greenspan.

of job insecurity in the high-tech economy, there was "[a] typical restraint on compensation increases." In 1996, even with a tight labor market, 46% of workers at large firms were fearful of layoffs — compared to only 25% in 1991, when unemployment was much higher.

> The reluctance of workers to leave their jobs to seek other employment as the labor market tightened has provided further evidence of such concern, as has the tendency toward longer labor union contracts. For many decades, contracts rarely exceeded three years. Today, one can point to five- and six-year contracts — contracts that are commonly characterized by an emphasis on job security and that involve only modest wage increases. The low level of work stoppages of recent years also attests to concern about job security.

Thus the willingness of workers in recent years to trade off smaller increases in wages for greater job security seems to be reasonably well documented. For the bosses, the high-tech economy is the next best thing to high unemployment for keeping our minds right. "Fighting inflation" translates operationally to increasing job insecurity and making workers less likely to strike or to look for new jobs.

Patents

The patent privilege has been used on a massive scale to promote concentration of capital, erect entry barriers, and maintain a monopoly of advanced technology in the hands of western corporations. It is hard even to imagine how much more decentralized the economy would be without it. Right-libertarian Murray Rothbard considered patents a fundamental violation of free market principles.

> The man who has not bought a machine and who arrives at the same invention independently, will, on the free market, be perfectly able to use and sell his invention. Patents prevent a man from using his invention even though all the property is his and he has not stolen the invention, either explicitly or implicitly, from the first inventor. Patents, therefore, are grants of exclusive monopoly privilege by the State and are invasions of property rights on the market.[45]

Patents make an astronomical price difference. Until the early 1970s, for example, Italy did not recognize drug patents. As a result, Roche Products charged the British national health a price over 40 times greater for patented components of Librium and Valium than charged by competitors in Italy.[46]

Patents suppress innovation as much as they encourage it. Chakravarthi Raghavan pointed out that research scientists who actually do the work of inventing are required to sign over patent rights as a condition of employment, while patents and industrial security programs prevent sharing of information, and suppress competition in further improvement of patented inventions.[47] Rothbard likewise argued that patents eliminate "the competitive spur for further

[45] *Man, Economy, and State*, vol. 2, 655.
[46] Raghavan, *Recolonization* 124.
[47] *Op. cit.* 118.

research" because incremental innovation based on others' patents is prohibited, and because the holder can "rest on his laurels for the entire period of the patent," with no fear of a competitor improving his invention. And they hamper technical progress because "mechanical inventions are discoveries of natural law rather than individual creations, and hence similar independent inventions occur all the time. The simultaneity of inventions is a familiar historical fact."[48]

The intellectual property regime under the Uruguay Round of GATT goes far beyond traditional patent law in suppressing innovation. One benefit of traditional patent law, at least, was that it required an invention under patent to be published. Under U.S. pressure, however, "trade secrets" were included in GATT. As a result, governments will be required to help suppress information not formally protected by patents.[49]

And patents are not necessary as an incentive to innovate. According to Rothbard, invention is rewarded by the competitive advantage accruing to the first developer of an idea. This is borne out by F. M. Scherer's testimony before the FTC in 1995.[50] Scherer spoke of a survey of 91 companies in which only seven "accorded high significance to patent protection as a factor in their R & D investments." Most of them described patents as "the least important of considerations." Most companies considered their chief motivation in R & D decisions to be "the necessity of remaining competitive, the desire for efficient production, and the desire to expand and diversify their sales." In another study, Scherer found no

[48] *Op. cit.* 655, 658-659.

[49] Raghavan, *op. cit.* 122.

[50] *Hearings on Global and Innovation-Based Competition.*

negative effect on R & D spending as a result of compulsory licensing of patents. A survey of U.S. firms found that 86% of inventions would have been developed without patents. In the case of automobiles, office equipment, rubber products, and textiles, the figure was 100%.

The one exception was drugs, in which 60% supposedly would not have been invented. I suspect disingenuousness on the part of the respondents, however. For one thing, drug companies get an unusually high portion of their R & D funding from the government, and many of their most lucrative products were developed entirely at government expense. And Scherer himself cited evidence to the contrary. The reputation advantage for being the first into a market is considerable. For example in the late 1970s, the structure of the industry and pricing behavior was found to be very similar between drugs with and those without patents. Being the first mover with a non-patented drug allowed a company to maintain a 30% market share and to charge premium prices.

The injustice of patent monopolies is exacerbated by government funding of research and innovation, with private industry reaping monopoly profits from technology it didn't spend a penny to develop. In 1999, extending the research and experimentation tax credit was, along with extensions of a number of other corporate tax preferences, considered the most urgent business of the Congressional leadership. Hastert, when asked if any elements of the tax bill were essential, said: "I think the [tax preference] extenders are something we're going to have to work on." Ways and Means Chair Bill Archer added, "before the year is out... we will do the extenders in a very stripped down bill that doesn't include anything else." A five-year extension of the research and experimentation credit (retroactive to 1 July 1999) was expected to cost $13.1 billion. (That credit makes the effective tax rate on R & D spending less than zero.)[51]

The Government Patent Policy Act of 1980, with 1984 and 1986 amendments, allowed private industry to keep patents on products developed with government R & D money — and then to charge ten, twenty, or forty times the cost of production. For example, AZT was developed with government money and in the public domain since 1964. The patent was given away to Burroughs Wellcome Corp.[52]

As if the deck were not sufficiently stacked already, the pharmaceutical companies in 1999 actually lobbied Congress to extend certain patents by two years by a special act of private law.[53]

Patents have been used throughout the twentieth century "to circumvent antitrutst laws," according to David Noble. They were "bought up in large numbers to suppress competition," which also resulted in "the suppression of invention itself."[54] Edwin Prindle, a corporate patent lawyer, wrote in 1906:

> Patents are the best and most effective means of controlling competition. They occasionally give absolute command of the market, enabling their owner to name the price without regard to the cost of production.... Patents are the only legal form of

[51]Citizens for Tax Justice, *GOP Leaders Distill Essence of Tax Plan.*
[52]Chris Lewis, "Public Assets, Private Profits."
[53]Benjamin Grove, "Gibbons Backs Drug-Monopoly Bill."
[54]*America by Design* 84-109.

absolute monopoly.[55]

Patents played a key role in the formation of the electrical appliance, communications, and chemical industries. G. E. and Westinghouse expanded to dominate the electrical manufacturing market at the turn of the century largely through patent control. In 1906 they curtailed the patent litigation between them by pooling their patents. AT&T also expanded "primarily through strategies of patent monopoly." The American chemical industry was marginal until 1917, when Attorney-General Mitchell Palmer seized German patents and distributed them among the major American chemical companies. DuPont got licenses on 300 of the 735 patents.[56]

Patents are also being used on a global scale to lock the transnational corporations into a permanent monopoly of productive technology. The single most totalitarian provision of the Uruguay Round is probably its "intellectual property" provisions. GATT has extended both the scope and duration of patents far beyond anything ever envisioned in original patent law. In England, patents were originally for fourteen years — the time needed to train two journeymen in succession (and by analogy, the time necessary to go into production and reap the initial profit for originality). By that standard, given the shorter training times required today, and the shorter lifespan of technology, the period of monopoly should be shorter. Instead, the U.S. seeks to extend them to fifty years.[57] According to Martin

[55] *America by Design* 90.
[56] *America by Design* 10, 16.
[57] Raghavan, *Recolonization* 119-120.

Khor Kok Peng, the U.S. is by far the most absolutist of the participants in the Uruguay Round. Unlike the European Community, and for biological processes for animal and plant protection.[58]

The provisions for biotech are really a way of increasing trade barriers, and forcing consumers to subsidize the TNCs engaged in agribusiness. The U.S. seeks to apply patents to genetically-modified organisms, effectively pirating the work of generations of Third World breeders by isolating beneficial genes in traditional varieties and incorporating them in new GMOs — and maybe even enforcing patent rights against the traditional variety which was the source of the genetic material. For example Monsanto has attempted to use the presence of their DNA in a crop as *prima facie* evidence of pirating — when it is much more likely that their variety cross-pollinated and contaminated the farmer's crop against his will. The Pinkerton agency, by the way, plays a leading role in investigating such charges — that's right, the same folks who have been breaking strikes and kicking organizers down stairs for the past century. Even jack-booted thugs have to diversify to make it in the global economy.

The developed world has pushed particularly hard to protect industries relying on or producing "generic technologies," and to restrict diffusion of "dual use" technologies. The U. S.-Japanese trade agreement on semi-conductors, for example, is a "cartel-like, 'managed trade' agreement." So much for "free trade."[59]

---

[58] *The Uruguay Round and Third World Sovereignty* 28.

[59] Dieter Ernst, "Technology, Economic Security and Latecomer Industrialization," in Raghavan 39-40.

Patent law traditionally required a holder to work the invention in a country in order to receive patent protection. U.K. law allowed compulsory licensing after three years if an invention was not being worked, or being worked fully, and demand was being met "to a substantial extent" by importation; or where the export market was not being supplied because of the patentee's refusal to grant licenses on reasonable terms.[60]

The central motivation in the GATT intellectual property regime, however, is to permanently lock in the collective monopoly of advanced technology by TNCs, and prevent independent competition from ever arising in the Third World. It would, as Martin Khor Kok Peng writes, "effectively prevent the diffusion of technology to the Third World, and would tremendously increase monopoly royalties of the TNCs whilst curbing the potential devel- opment of Third World technology." Only one percent of patents worldwide are owned in the Third World. Of patents granted in the 1970s by Third World countries, 84% were foreign-owned. But fewer than 5% of foreign-owned patents were actually used in production. As we saw before, the purpose of owning a patent is not necessarily to use it, but to prevent anyone else from using it.[61]

Raghavan summed up nicely the effect on the Third World:

> Given the vast outlays in R and D and investments, as well as the short life cycle of some of these products, the leading Industrial Nations are trying to

[60] Raghavan 120, 138.
[61] *Op. cit.* 29-30.

> prevent emergence of competition by controlling... the flows of technology to others. The Uruguay round is being sought to be used to create export monopolies for the products of Industrial Nations, and block or slow down the rise of competitive rivals, particularly in the newly industrializing Third World countries. At the same time the technologies of senescent industries of the north are sought to be exported to the South under conditions of assured rentier income.[62]

Corporate propagandists piously denounce anti-globalists as enemies of the Third World, seeking to use trade barriers to maintain an affluent Western lifestyle at the expense of the poor nations. The above measures — trade barriers — to permanently suppress Third World technology and keep the South as a big sweatshop, give the lie to this "humanitarian" concern. This is not a case of differing opinions, or of sincerely mistaken understanding of the facts. Setting aside false subtleties, what we see here is pure evil at work — Orwell's "boot stamping on a human face forever." If any architects of this policy believe it to be for general human well-being, it only shows the capacity of ideology to justify the oppressor to himself and enable him to sleep at night.

Infrastructure

Spending on transportation and communications networks from general revenues, rather than from taxes and user fees, allows big business to "externalize its costs" on the

[62] *Op. cit.* 96.

public, and conceal its true operating expenses. Chomsky described this state capitalist underwriting of shipping costs quite accurately:

> One well-known fact about trade is that it's highly subsidized with huge market-distorting factors.... The most obvious is that every form of transport is highly subsidized.... Since trade naturally requires transport, the costs of transport enter into the calculation of the efficiency of trade. But there are huge subsidies to reduce the costs of transport, through manipulation of energy costs and all sorts of market-distorting functions.[63]

Every wave of concentration of capital has followed a publicly subsidized infrastructure system of some sort. The national railroad system, built largely on free or below-cost land donated by the government, was followed by concentration in heavy industry, petrochemicals, and finance. The next major infrastructure projects were the national highway system, starting with the system of designated national highways in the 1920s and culminating with Eisenhower's interstate system; and the civil aviation system, built almost entirely with federal money. The result was massive concentration in retail, agriculture, and food processing.

The third such project was the infrastructure of the worldwide web, originally built by the Pentagon. It permits, for the first time, direction of global operations in real time from a single corporate headquarters, and is accelerating the concentration of capital on a global scale. To quote Chomsky again,

---

[63] "How Free is the Free Market?"

> The telecommunications revolution... is... another state component of the international economy that didn't develop through private capital, but through the public paying to destroy themselves...[64]

The centralized corporate economy depends for its existence on a shipping price system which is artificially distorted by government intervention. To fully grasp how dependent the corporate economy is on socializing transportation and communications costs, imagine what would happen if truck and aircraft fuel were taxed enough to pay the full cost of maintenance and new building costs on highways and airports; and if fossil fuels depletion allowances were removed. The result would be a massive increase in shipping costs. Does anyone seriously believe that Wal-Mart could continue to undersell local retailers, or corporate agribusiness could destroy the family farm?

Intellectually honest right-libertarians freely admit as much. For example, Tiber Machan wrote in *The Freeman* that

> Some people will say that stringent protection of rights [against eminent domain] would lead to small airports, at best, and many constraints on construction. Of course — but what's so wrong with that?
>
> Perhaps the worst thing about modern industrial life has been the power of political authorities to grant special privileges to some enterprises to violate the rights of third parties whose permission would be too expensive to obtain. The need to obtain that permission would indeed seriously impede what most

[64] *Class Warfare* 40.

> environmentalists see as rampant — indeed reckless — industrialization.
>
> The system of private property rights — in which... all... kinds of... human activity must be conducted within one's own realm except where cooperation from others has been gained voluntarily — is the greatest moderator of human aspirations.... In short, people may reach goals they aren't able to reach with their own resources only by convincing others, through arguments and fair exchanges, to cooperate.[65]

The logjams and bottlenecks in the transportation system are an inevitable result of subsidies. Those who debate the reason for planes stacked up at O'Hare airport, or decry the fact that highways and bridges are deteriorating several times faster than repairs are being budgeted, need only read an economics 101 text. Market prices are signals that relate supply to demand. When subsidies distort these signals, the consumer does not perceive the real cost of producing the goods he consumes. The "feedback loop" is broken, and demands on the system overwhelm it beyond its ability to respond. When people don't have to pay the real cost of something they consume, they aren't very careful about only using what they need.

It is interesting that every major antitrust action in this century has involved either some basic energy resource, or some form of infrastructure, on which the overall economy depends. Standard Oil, AT&T, and Microsoft were all cases in which monopoly price gouging was a danger to the economy as a whole. This brings to mind Engels' observation

[65] "On Airports and Individual Rights."

that advanced capitalism would reach a stage where the state — "the official representative of capitalist society" — would have to convert "the great institutions for intercourse and communication" into state property. Engels did not foresee the use of antitrust actions to achieve the same end.[66]

"Military Keynesianism"

The leading sectors of the economy, including cybernetics, communications, and military industry, have their sales and profits virtually guaranteed by the state. The entire manufacturing sector, as a whole, was permanently expanded beyond recognition by an infusion of federal money during World War II. In 1939 the entire manufacturing plant of the U.S. was valued at $40 billion. By 1945, another $26 billion worth of plant and equipment had been built, "two thirds of it paid for directly from government funds." The top 250 corporations in 1939 owned 65% of plant and equipment, but during the war operated 79% of all new facilities built with government funds.[67]

Machine tools were vastly expanded by the war. In 1940, 23% of machine tools in use were less than 10 years old. By 1945, the figure had grown to 62%. The industry contracted rapidly after 1945, and would probably have gone into a depression, had it not returned to wartime levels of output during Korea and remained that way throughout the Cold War. The R & D complex, likewise, was a creation of the war. Between 1939 and 1945, the share of AT&T

[66] *Anti-Duhring.*

[67] Mills, *The Power Elite* 101.

research expenditures made up of government contracts expanded from 1% to 83%. Over 90% of the patents resulting from government-funded wartime research were given away to industry. The modern electronics industry was largely a product of World War II and Cold War spending (e.g., miniaturization of circuits for bomb proximity fuses, high capacity computers for command and control, etc.).[68]

The jumbo jet industry would never have come about without continuous Cold War levels of military spending. The machine tools needed for producing large aircraft were so complex and expensive that no "small peacetime orders" would have provided a sufficient production run to pay for them. Without large military orders, they would simply not have existed. The aircraft industry quickly spiraled into red ink after 1945, and was near bankruptcy at the beginning of the 1948 war scare, after which Truman restored it to life with massive spending. By 1964, 90% of aerospace R & D was funded by the government, with massive spillover into the electronics, machine tool, and other industries.[69]

Other Subsidies

Infrastructure and military spending are not the only examples of the process by which cost and risk are socialized, and profit is privatized — or, as Rothbard put it, by which "our corporate state uses the coercive taxing power either to accumulate corporate capital or to lower corporate costs."[70]

[68]Noble, *Forces of Production* 8-16.

[69]Noble, *Forces of Production* 6-7; Kofsky, *Harry S. Truman and the War Scare of 1948.*

[70]"Confessions of a Right-Wing Liberal."

Some of these government assumptions of risk and cost are ad hoc and targeted toward specific industries.

Among the greatest beneficiaries of such underwriting are electrical utilities. Close to 100% of all research and development for nuclear power is either performed by the government itself, in its military reactor program, or by lump-sum R & D grants; the government waives use-charges for nuclear fuels, subsidizes uranium production, provides access to government land below market price (and builds hundreds of miles of access roads at taxpayer expense), enriches uranium, and disposes of waste at sweetheart prices. The Price-Anderson Act of 1957 limited the liability of the nuclear power industry, and assumed government liability above that level.[71] A Westinghouse official admitted in 1953,

> If you were to inquire whether Westinghouse might consider putting up its own money.., we would have to say "No." The cost of the plant would be a question mark until after we built it and, by that sole means, found out the answer. We would not be sure of successful plant operation until after we had done all the work and operated successfully.... This is still a situation of pyramiding uncertainties.... There is a distinction between risk-taking and recklessness.[72]

So much for profit as a reward for the entrepreneur's risk. These "entrepreneurs" make their profits in the same way as a seventeenth-century courtier, by obtaining the favor of the king. To quote Chomsky,

---

[71] Adams and Brock 279-281.

[72] *Ibid.* 278-279.

> The sectors of the economy that remain competitive are those that feed from the public trough.... The glories of Free Enterprise provide a useful weapon against government policies that might benefit the general population.... But the rich and powerful... have long appreciated the need to protect themselves from the destructive forces of free-market capitalism, which may provide suitable themes for rousing oratory, but only so long as the public handout and the regulatory and protectionist apparatus are secure, and state power is on call when needed,[73]

Dwayne Andreas, the CEO of Archer Daniels Midland, admitted that "[t]here is not one grain of anything in the world that is sold in the free market. Not one. The only place you see a free market is in the speeches of politicians."[74]

Big business also enjoys financial support through the tax code. It is likely that most of the Fortune 500 would go bankrupt without corporate welfare. Direct federal tax breaks to business in 1996 were close to $350 billion.[75] This figure, for federal corporate welfare alone, is over two-thirds of annual corporate profits for 1996 ($460 billion).[76]

Estimates of state and local tax breaks is fairly impressionistic, since they vary not only with each critic's subjective definition of "corporate welfare," but involve the tax codes of fifty states and the public records of thousands of municipalities. Besides money pimps in the state and local

[73]Chomsky, *Deterring Democracy* 144.

[74]Don Carney, "Dwayne's World."

[75]Based on my crunching on numbers in Zepezauer and Naiman, *Take the Rich Off Welfare.*

[76]*Statistical Abstract of the United States* 1996.

governments are embarrassed by the sweet deals they give their corporate johns. In my own state of Arkansas, the incorruptible Baptist preacher who serves as governor opposed a bill to require quarterly public reports from the Department of Economic Development on its special tax breaks to businesses. "[K]eeping incentive records from public scrutiny is important in attracting business," and releasing "proprietary information" could have a "chilling effect."[77] But state and local corporate welfare could easily amount to a figure comparable to federal.

Taken as a whole, direct tax breaks to business at all levels of government are probably on the same order of magnitude as corporate profits. And this understates the effect of corporate welfare, since it disproportionately goes to a handful of giant firms in each industry. For example, accelerated depreciation favors expansion by existing firms. New firms find it of little benefit, since they are likely to lose money their first few years. An established firm, however, can run a loss in a new venture and charge the accelerated depreciation against its profits on old facilities.[78]

The most outrageous of these tax expenditures is the subsidy to the actual financial transactions by which capital is concentrated. The interest deduction on corporate debt, most of which was run up on leveraged buyouts and acquisitions, costs the treasury over $200 billion a year.[79] Without this deduction, the wave of mergers in the 1980s, or the megamergers of the 1990s, could never have taken place. On top of everything else, this acts as a massive direct

[77] *Arkansas Democrat-Gazette* 3 Feb. 2001.

[78] Baratz, "Corporate Giants and the Power Structure."

[79] Zepezauer 122-123.

subsidy to banking, increasing the power of finance capital in the corporate economy to a level greater than it has been since the Age of Morgan.

A closely related subsidy is the exemption from capital gains of securities transactions involved in corporate mergers (i.e. "stock swaps") — even though premiums are usually paid well over the market value of the stock.[80] The 1986 tax reform included a provision which prevented corporations from deducting fees for investment 'banks and advisers involved in leveraged buyouts. The 1996 minimum wage increase repealed this provision, with one exception: interest deductions were removed for employee buyouts.[81]

Right-libertarians like Rothbard object to classifying tax expenditures as subsidies. It presumes that tax money rightfully belongs to the government, when in fact the government is only letting them keep what is rightfully theirs. The tax code is indeed unfair, but the solution is to eliminate the taxes for everyone, not to level the code up.[82] This is a very shaky argument. Supporters of tax code reform in the 1980s insisted that the sole legitimate purpose of taxation was to raise revenue, not to provide carrots and sticks for social engineering purposes. And, semantic quibbling aside, the current tax system would be exactly the same if we started out with zero tax rates and then imposed a punitive tax only on those not engaged in favored activities. Either way, the uneven tax policy gives a competitive advantage to privileged industries.

---

[80] Green 11.

[81] Judis, "Bare Minimum."

[82] Rothbard, *Power and Market* 104.

Political Repression

In times of unusual popular consciousness and mobilization, when the capitalist system faces grave political threats, the state resorts to repression until the danger is past. The major such waves in this country — the Haymarket reaction, and the red scares after the world wars — are recounted by Goldstein.[83] But the wave of repression which began in the 1970s, though less intense, has been permanently institutionalized to a unique extent.

Until the late 1960s, elite perspective was governed by the New Deal social contract. The corporate state would buy stability and popular acquiescence in imperialist exploitation abroad by guaranteeing a level of prosperity and security to the middle class. In return for higher wages, unions would enforce management control of the workplace. But starting during the Vietnam era, the elite's thinking underwent a profound change.

They concluded from the 1960s experience that the social contract had failed. In response to the antiwar protests and race riots, LBJ and Nixon began to create an institutional framework for martial law, to make sure that any such disorder in the future could be dealt with differently. Johnson's operation GARDEN PLOT involved domestic surveillance by the military, contingency plans for military cooperation with local police in suppressing disorder in all fifty states, plans for mass preventive detention, and joint exercises of police and the regular military.[84] Governor Reagan and his National Guard chief Louis Giuffrida were enthusiastic sup-

[83] *Political Repression in Modern America.*

[84] Morales, *U.S. Military Civil Disturbance Planning.*

porters of GARDEN PLOT exercises in California. Reagan was also a pioneer in creating quasi-military SWAT teams, which now exist in every major town.

The wave of wildcat strikes in the early 1970s showed that organized labor could no longer keep its part of the bargain, and that the social contract should be reassessed. At the same time, the business press was flooded with articles on the impending "capital shortage," and calls for shifting resources from consumption to capital accumulation. They predicted frankly that a cap on real wages would be hard to force on the public in the existing political environment.[85] This sentiment was expressed by Huntington et al. in The Crisis of Democracy (a paper for the Trilateral Institution — a good proxy for elite thinking); they argued that the system was collapsing from demand overload, because of an excess of democracy.

Corporations embraced the full range of union-busting possibilities in Taft-Hartley, risking only token fines from the NLRB. They drastically increased management resources devoted to workplace surveillance and control, a necessity because of discontent from stagnant wages and mounting workloads.[86] Wages as a percentage of value added have declined drastically since the 1970s; all increases in labor productivity have been channeled into profit and investment, rather than wages. A new Cold War military buildup further transferred public resources to industry.

A series of events like the fall of Saigon, the nonaligned movement, and the New International Economic Order were taken as signs that the transnational corporate empire was

[85] Boyte, *Backyard Revolution* 13-16.

[86] *Fat and Mean.*

losing control. Reagan's escalating intervention in Central America was a partial response to this perception. But more importantly the Uruguay Round of GATT snatched total victory from the jaws of defeat; it ended all barriers to TNCs buying up entire economies, locked the west into monopoly control of modern technology, and created a world government on behalf of global corporations.

In the meantime the U.S. was, in the words of Richard K. Moore, importing techniques of social control from the imperial periphery to the core area. With the help of the Drug War and the National Security State, the apparatus of repression continued to grow. The Drug War has turned the Fourth Amendment into toilet paper; civil forfeiture, with the aid of jailhouse snitches, gives police the power to steal property without ever filing charges — a lucrative source of funds for helicopters and kevlar vests. SWAT teams have led to the militarization of local police forces, and cross-training with the military has led many urban police departments to view the local population as an occupied enemy.[87]

Reagan's crony Giuffrida resurfaced as head of FEMA, where he worked with Oliver North to fine-tune GARDEN PLOT. North, as the NSC liaison with FEMA from 1982-84, developed a plan "to suspend the constitution in the event of a national crisis, such as nuclear war, violent and widespread internal dissent or national opposition to a U.S. military invasion abroad."[88] GARDEN PLOT, interestingly, was implemented during the Rodney King Riots and in recent anti-globalization protests. Delta Force provided intelligence

[87] Weber, *Warrior Cops.*

[88] Chardy, "Reagan Aides and the 'Secret' Government."

and advice in those places and at Waco.[89]

Another innovation is to turn everyone we deal with into a police agent. Banks routinely report "suspicious" movements of cash; under "know your customer" programs, retailers report purchases of items which can conceivably be used in combination to manufacture drugs; libraries come under pressure to report on readers of "subversive" material; DARE programs turn kids into police informers.

Computer technology has increased the potential for surveillance to Orwellian levels. Pentium III processors were revealed to embed identity codes in every document written on them. Police forces are experimenting with combinations of public cameras, digital face-recognition technology, and databases of digital photos. Image Data LLC, a company in the process of buying digital drivers license photos from all fifty states, was exposed as a front for the Secret Service.

Conclusion

It is almost too easy to bring back Bob Novak and Secretary O'Neill for another kick — but I can't resist. "Marxist class warfare?" "Robber baron rhetoric?" Well, the pages above recount the "class warfare" waged by the robber barons themselves. If their kind tend to squeal like pigs when we talk about class, it's because they've been stuck. But all the squealing in the world won't change the facts.

But what are the implications of the above facts for our movement? It is commonly acknowledged that the manorial economy was founded on force. Although you will never see

[89]Rosenberg, *The Empire Strikes Back*; Cockburn, *The Jackboot State.*

the issue addressed by Milton Friedman, intellectually honest right libertarians like Rothbard acknowledge the role of the state in creating European feudalism and American slavery. Rothbard, drawing the obvious conclusion from this fact, acknowledged the right of peasants or freed slaves to take over their "forty acres and a mule" without compensation to the landlord.

But we have seen that industrial capitalism, to the same extent as manorialism or slavery, was founded on force. Like its predecessors, capitalism could not have survived at any point in its history without state intervention. Coercive state measures at every step have denied workers access to capital, forced them to sell their labor in a buyer's market, and protected the centers of economic power from the dangers of the free market. To quote Benjamin Tucker again, landlords and capitalists cannot extract surplus value from labor without the help of the state. The modern worker, like the slave or the serf, is the victim of ongoing robbery; he works in an enterprise built from past stolen labor. By the same principles that Rothbard recognized in the agrarian realm, the modern worker is justified in taking direct control of production, and keeping the entire product of his labor.

In a very real sense, every subsidy and privilege described above is a form of slavery. Slavery, simply put, is the use of coercion to live off of someone else's labor. For example, consider the worker who pays $300 a month for a drug under patent, that would cost $30 in a free market. If he is paid $15 an hour, the eighteen hours he works every month to pay the difference are slavery. Every hour worked to pay usury on a credit card or mortgage is slavery. The hours worked to pay unnecessary distribution and marketing costs (comprising half of retail prices), because of subsidies to economic centralization, is slavery. Every additional hour someone works to meet his basic needs, because the state tilts the field in favor of the bosses and forces him to sell his labor for less than it is worth, is slavery.

All these forms of slavery together probably amount to half our working hours. If we kept the full value of our labor, we could probably maintain current levels of consumption with a work week of twenty hours. As Bill Haywood said, "for every man who gets a dollar he didn't sweat for, someone else sweated to produce a dollar he never received."

Our survey also casts doubt on the position of "anarchist" social democrat Noam Chomsky, who is notorious for his distinction between "visions" and "goals." His long-term vision is a decentralized society of self-governing communities and workplaces, loosely federated together — the traditional anarchist vision. His immediate goal, however, is to strengthen the regulatory state in order to break up "private concentrations of power," before anarchism can be achieved. But if, as we have seen, capitalism is dependent on the state to guarantee its survival, it follows that it is sufficient to eliminate the statist props to capitalism. In a letter of 4 September 1867, Engels aptly summed up the difference between anarchists and state socialists: "They say 'abolish the state and capital will go to the devil.' We propose the reverse." Exactly.

CHAPTER

FOUR

THE SUBSIDY OF HISTORY

KEVIN CARSON

A considerable number of libertarian commentators have remarked on the sheer scale of subsidies and protections to big business, on their structural importance to the existing form of corporate capitalism, and on the close intermeshing of corporate and state interests in the present state capitalist economy. We pay less attention, however, to the role of past state coercion, in previous centuries, in laying the structural foundations of the present system. The extent to which present-day concentrations of wealth and corporate power are the legacy of past injustice, I call the subsidy of history.

The first and probably the most important subsidy of history is land theft, by which peasant majorities were deprived of their just property rights and turned into tenants forced to pay rent based on the artificial "property" titles of

https://c4ss.org/content/13192

state-privileged elites. Of course, all such artificial titles not founded on appropriation by individual labor are completely illegitimate.

As Ludwig von Mises pointed out in *Socialism*, the normal functioning of the market never results in a state of affairs in which most of the land of a country is "owned" by a tiny class of absentee landlords and the peasant majority pay rent for the land they work. Wherever it is found, it is the result of past coercion and robbery.

Murray Rothbard, in *The Ethics of Liberty*, explained the injustice of feudal landlordism:

> But suppose that centuries ago, Smith was tilling the soil and therefore legitimately owning the land; and then that Jones came along and settled down near Smith, claiming by use of coercion the title to Smith's land, and extracting payment or "rent" from Smith for the privilege of continuing to till the soil. Suppose that now, centuries later, Smith's descendants (or, for that matter, other unrelated families) are now tilling the soil, while Jones's descendants, or those who purchased their claims, still continue to exact tribute from the modern tillers. Where is the true property right in such a case? It should be clear that here . . . we have a case of continuing aggression against the true owners – the true possessors – of the land, the tillers, or peasants, by the illegitimate owner, the man whose original and continuing claim to the land and its fruits has come from coercion and violence. Just as the original Jones was a continuing aggressor against the original Smith, so the modern peasants are being aggressed against by the modern holder of the Jones-derived land title. In this case of

> what we might call "feudalism" or "land monopoly," the feudal or monopolist landlords have no legitimate claim to the property. The current "tenants," or peasants, should be the absolute owners of their property, and, as in the case of slavery, the land titles should be transferred to the peasants, without compensation to the monopoly landlords.

So rather than defending all existing land titles in the name of the "sanctity of property" and protesting when some left-wing government institutes a land reform that transfers feudal land titles to the peasantry, Rothbard favored 1) dividing up Southern plantations and giving freed American slaves "forty acres and a mule," and 2) transferring the latifundia from Latin American landed oligarchies to the peasants.

In the Old World, especially Britain (where the Industrial Revolution began), the expropriation of the peasant majority by a politically dominant landed oligarchy took place over several centuries in the late medieval and early modern period. It began with the enclosure of the open fields in the late Middle Ages. Under the Tudors, Church fiefdoms (especially monastic lands) were expropriated by the state and distributed among the landed aristocracy. The new "owners" evicted or rack-rented the peasants.

Expropriating from the Peasantry

The Restoration Parliament of the seventeenth century carried out a series of land "reforms" that abolished feudal land tenure altogether – but only upward. There were two ways Parliament could have abolished feudalism and reformed property. It might have treated the customary possessive rights of the peasantry as genuine title to property in the modern sense, and then abolished their rents. But what it actually did, instead, was to treat the artificial "property rights" of the landed aristocracy, in feudal legal theory, as real property rights in the modern sense; the landed classes were given full legal title, and the peasants were transformed into tenants at will with no customary restriction on the rents that could be charged. The most important component of this "reform" was the Statute of Frauds of 1677, which nullified rights of copyhold by making them unenforceable in royal courts.

Finally, the Parliamentary Enclosures of the eighteenth and early nineteenth century robbed the peasantry of their rights of common. The propertied classes of England saw the economic independence provided by the commons as a threat, first to an adequate supply of agricultural wage labor on the landed oligarchy's own land, and later to an adequate supply of factory labor willing to work the long hours and low pay demanded by the owners. The literature of the propertied classes of the time was quite explicit on their motivation: the laboring classes would not work hard enough or cheaply enough so long as they had independent access to the means of subsistence. They had to be made as poor and hungry as possible so that they would be willing to accept work on whatever terms it was offered.

A version of the same phenomenon took place in the Third World. In European colonies where a large native peasantry already lived, states sometimes granted quasi-feudal titles to landed elites to collect rent from those already living on and cultivating the land; a good example is latifundismo, which prevails in Latin America to the present day. Another example is British East Africa. The most fertile 20 percent of Kenya was stolen by the colonial authorities, and the native peasantry evicted, so the land could be used for cash-crop farming by white settlers (using the labor of the evicted peasantry, of course, to work their own former land). As for those who remained on their own land, they were "encouraged" to enter the wage-labor market by a stiff poll tax that had to be paid in cash. Multiply these examples by a hundred and you get a bare hint of the sheer scale of robbery over the past 500 years.

Contrary to Mises's rosy version of the Industrial Revolution in *Human Action*, factory owners were not innocent in all of this. Mises claimed that the capital investments on which the factory system was built came largely from hardworking and thrifty workmen who saved their own earnings as investment capital. In fact, however, they were junior partners of the landed elites, with much of their investment capital coming either from the Whig landed oligarchy or from the overseas fruits of mercantilism, slavery, and colonialism.

In addition, factory employers depended on harsh authoritarian measures by the government to keep labor under control and reduce its bargaining power. In England the Laws of Settlement acted as a sort of internal passport system, preventing workers from traveling outside the parish of their birth without government permission. Thus workers were prevented from "voting with their feet" in search of better-paying jobs. You might think this would have worked to the disadvantage of employers in underpopulated areas, like Manchester and other areas of the industrial north. But never fear: the state came to the employers' rescue. Because workers were forbidden to migrate on their own in search of better pay, employers were freed from the necessity of offering high enough wages to attract free agents; instead, they were able to "hire" workers auctioned off by the parish Poor Law authorities on terms set by collusion between the authorities and employers.

Legalized Discrimination Against Laborers

The Combination Laws, which prevented workers from freely associating to bargain with employers, were enforced entirely by administrative law without any protections of common-law due process. And they were only enforced against combination by workers, not against combination by employers (such as blacklisting "troublemakers" and collusive setting of wages). The Riot Act (1714) and other police-state legislation during the Napoleonic Wars were used to stem the threat of domestic revolution, essentially turning the English working class into an occupied enemy population. Such legislation criminalized most forms of association.

Even fraternal associations for mutual aid, burial and sick benefits, and the like operated in the face of hostility from the state, according to historians of the friendly-society movement such as Bob James and Peter Gray. Under the terms of the Combination Act, friendly societies were subjected to close judicial supervision lest direct craft production be organized for barter among the unemployed, or the societies' benefits cross the line and function as de facto unemployment insurance for striking workers. The Corresponding Societies Act, passed around the same time, prohibited all societies that administered secret oaths or were federated on a national scale.

So the Industrial Revolution was, in fact, built on a system of legal peonage in which employers were directly implicated. The form taken by the factory system surely reflects this history. In a Britain composed of peasant smallholders, with no restraints on free association, workers would have been free to mobilize their own properties as capital through mutual credit institutions. Absentee ownership and hierarchy would likely have been far, far less prevalent, and the factory system where it existed far less oppressive and authoritarian.

A similar process occurred in the colonization of settler societies like America and Australia, by which the colonial powers and their landed elites attempted to replicate feudal patterns of property ownership. In such colonies, the state preempted ownership of vacant land and restricted working people's access to it. Sometimes they gave title to vacant land to privileged land speculators, who were able to charge rent to those who homesteaded it (the legitimate owners).

E. G. Wakefield, an early nineteenth-century British theorist of colonialism, advocated just such preemption on the same grounds that the propertied and employing classes of Britain had supported Enclosure: it was easier to hire labor on favorable terms to the employer. In England and America, he wrote:

> In colonies, labourers for hire are scarce. The scarcity of labourers for hire is the universal complaint of colonies. It is the one cause, both of the high wages which put the colonial labourer at his ease, and of the exorbitant wages which sometimes harass the capitalist...

> Where land is cheap and all men are free, where every one who so pleases can obtain a piece of land for himself, not only is labour very dear, as respects the labourers' share of the product, but the difficulty is to obtain combined labour at any price.

Consequently, "[f]ew, even of those whose lives are unusually long, can accumulate great masses of wealth."

Wakefield's disciple, Thomas Merivale, wrote of the "urgent desire for cheaper and more subservient labourers – for a class to whom the capitalist might dictate terms, instead of being dictated to by them."

Land preemption was a major element of colonial policy in early American history. Gary Nash, in *Class and Society in Early America*, described land grants in colonial America comparable to those of William I in England after the Conquest. In New York, for example, the largest estates granted by the British colonial administration (after the New Netherlands was acquired in the Dutch Wars) ranged from the hundreds of thousands to over a million acres. Governors continued to grant tracts of land in the hundreds of thousands of acres to their favorites, well into the eighteenth century. Under Governor Fletcher, some three-quarters of available land was granted to 30 persons.

Albert Jay Nock, in *Our Enemy, the State*, argued that "from the time of the first colonial settlement to the present day, America has been regarded as a practically limitless field for speculation in rental values." Many leading figures in the late colonial and early republican period were prominent investors in the great land companies, including George Washington in the Ohio, Mississippi, and Potomac Companies; Patrick Henry in the Yazoo Company; Benjamin

Franklin in the Vandalia Company, and so forth.

In *The Ethics of Liberty*, Rothbard condemned such pre-emption ("land-engrossing, where arbitrary claims to virgin land are used to keep first-transformers out of that land") on the same grounds that he criticized feudal landlordism. He called for voiding all current titles to vacant and unimproved land, and opening it up to free homesteading. In addition, in cases where current mortgage holders and landlords trace their title to state grants of land, the proper claim lies with those who first homesteaded the land, or their heirs and assigns.

The Homestead Act of 1862, an apparent exception to this general trend, was really just another illustration of it. The majority of land, rather than being claimed under the terms of the Homestead Act, was auctioned to the highest bidder. Even for land covered by the Act, according to Howard Zinn, the $200 fee was beyond the reach of many. As a result, much of the land was not homesteaded on Lockean principles at all, but initially went to speculators before being partitioned and resold to homesteaders. And compared to the 50 million acres covered by homestead legislation, 100 million acres were given away as railroad land grants during the Civil War – free of charge! In other words, the privileged classes got the gravy, and ordinary homesteaders got the bone.

Keeping the System Going

What I have described here are only the initial acts of coercion and robbery on which our existing form of industrial capitalism was founded. Of course it didn't stop there. Once the system was up and running, it depended on the state's ongoing efforts to maintain a legal structure of privilege, based on artificial property rights and artificial scarcity: enforcement of absentee titles to vacant and unimproved land; entry barriers for the banking industry to make credit artificially expensive and scarce; the artificial property rights of patent and copyright; and more. And starting in the late nineteenth century the modern form of corporate capitalism depended on even more massive state intervention: subsidies to long-distance shipping to make market areas and firm size artificially large; the cartelizing effects of patents and tariffs; regulatory cartelization; and entire industries and sectors of the economy either brought into existence or guaranteed a taxpayer-funded market by the post-1941 perpetual war economy.

Contrary to popular mythology, the New Deal was not a departure from some preexisting idyllic state of "laissez faire." There never was anything remotely approaching laissez faire. Capitalism—that is, the existing historical system as it actually developed—has had very little to do with free markets and a great deal to do with robbery and coercion. This is not to say that all avenues to economic advancement through independent entrepreneurship have been closed off. But it's much more of an uphill struggle than it would be in a free market, and the field is unfairly tilted in favor of the big players. In seeking to institute a genuine free market, libertarians shouldn't lose sight of these facts. What lessons are libertarians to learn from the previous historical account? First, there is nothing "libertarian" about the instinctive tendency to rally to the defense of existing property titles without regard to justice. As Karl Hess said in *The Libertarian Forum*, back in 1969,

> [L]ibertarianism wants to advance principles of property but . . . it in no way wishes to defend. . . all property which now is called private. Much of that property is stolen. Much is of dubious title. All of it is deeply intertwined with an immoral, coercive state system which has condoned, built on, and profited from slavery; has expanded through and exploited a brutal and aggressive imperial and colonial foreign policy, and continues to hold the people in a roughly serf-master relationship to political-economic power concentrations.

Second, in advocating free-market reform, we must consider the role of this historical legacy of injustice (the subsidy of history) in determining the winners under the present system. A "free-market reform" that simply locks in the beneficiaries of past robbery and privilege, and ratifies the past theft from which they benefit, will merely reward injustice and secure its ill-gotten gains.

From a libertarian ethical standpoint, the standard model of "privatization" (selling off state property to a large, politically connected private corporation, on terms most advantageous to the corporation) is therefore highly dubious. That's especially true considering that much of the property was created in the first place – at taxpayer expense – for the primary purpose of subsidizing the operating costs of big business. Much of the state-owned utility and transportation infrastructure in the Third World was created, at the behest of transnational financial elites, as a precondition for profitable Western capital investment. And the odious debt thus incurred, often by corrupt dictatorships acting in collusion with global finance, is then used by the World Bank to blackmail those countries into selling off their infrastructure to the very same transnational corporations it was created to benefit – usually at pennies on the dollar.

An Appropriate Model for Privatization

Rothbard's model of privatization is far superior: to void state titles to property and treat it as unowned, subject to immediate homesteading by those actually mixing their labor with it. That would mean that state universities would be transformed into the property of their students or faculty, as consumer or producer cooperatives. Government-owned utilities would become consumer cooperatives owned by ratepayers, and state-owned factories would be handed over to the work force and reorganized as worker cooperatives.

We must also be wary of pseudo-Coasean arguments that it "doesn't matter" who the property was originally stolen from, because it will end up in the hands of the "most efficient" owner. That's essentially the same argument used for eminent domain. Regardless of whose hands the property winds up in, the rightful owners and their descendants – who never received compensation – are out the value of what was stolen from them. And even the most inefficient ways of organizing production are pretty "efficient," comparatively speaking, when you have the competitive advantage of working with stolen property.

Besides, there is no such thing as generic "efficiency"; efficiency depends on the owner's purpose. The most efficient technique for subsistence farming on a small plot – economizing on land by building soil and adding intensive labor inputs – is entirely different from that for a feudal oligarch producing cash crops with access to more stolen land than he could possibly use, and often holding a majority of his stolen land out of use altogether. In any case, the rightful owner would no doubt find it far more "efficient" to be feeding himself on his own land, than starving in a shantytown because he can't afford to buy even the cheapest food from those "efficient" plantations occupying his stolen land.

The actual system of political economy that so many corporate apologists refer to as "our free market system" has in fact been characterized from the beginning by robbery. We must beware of "free market reforms" carried out by the robbers. They amount in practice to allowing the robbers – hands still full of loot – to say: "All right, no more stealing, starting . . . now!"

CHAPTER

FIVE

ECONOMIC CALCULATION IN THE CORPORATE COMMONWEALTH

KEVIN CARSON

The general lines of Ludwig von Mises's rational-calculation argument are well known. A market in factors of production is necessary for pricing production inputs so that a planner may allocate them rationally. The problem has nothing to do either with the volume of data or with agency problems. The question, rather, as Peter Klein put it, is "[h]ow does the principal know what to tell the agent to do?"

This calculation argument can be applied not only to a state-planned economy, but also to the internal planning of the large corporation under interventionism, or state capitalism. (By state capitalism, I refer to the means by which, as Murray Rothbard said, "our corporate state uses the coercive taxing power either to accumulate corporate capital or to

https://c4ss.org/content/14497

lower corporate costs," in addition to cartelizing markets through regulations, enforcing artificial property rights like "intellectual property," and otherwise protecting privilege against competition.)

Rothbard developed the economic calculation argument in just this way. He argued that the further removed the internal transfer pricing of a corporation became from real market prices, the more internal allocation of resources was characterized by calculational chaos.

Mises's calculation argument can be applied to the large corporation – both under state capitalism and to some extent in the free market – in another way not considered by Rothbard. The basic cause of calculational chaos, as Mises understood it, was the separation of entrepreneurial from technical knowledge and the attempt to make production decisions based on technical considerations alone, without regard to such entrepreneurial considerations as factor pricing. But the principle also works the other way: production decisions based solely on input and product prices, without regard to the details of production (the typical MBA practice of considering only finance and marketing, while treating the production process as a black box), also result in calculational chaos.

The chief focus of this article, however, is Mises's calculation argument in the light of distributed information. F. A. Hayek, in "The Uses of Knowledge in Society," raised a new problem: not the generation or source of data, but the sheer volume of data to be processed. In so doing, he is commonly understood to have opened a second front in Mises's war against state planning. But in fact his argument was almost as damaging to Mises as to the collectivists.

Mises minimized the importance of distributed information in his own criticisms of state planning. He denied any correlation between bureaucratization and large size in themselves. Bureaucracy as such was a particular rules-based approach to policy-making, in contrast to the profit-driven behavior of the entrepreneur. The private firm, therefore, was by definition exempt from the problem of bureaucracy.

In so arguing, he ignored the information and coordination problems inherent in large size. The large corporation necessarily distributes the knowledge relevant to informed entrepreneurial decisions among many departments and subdepartments until the cost of aggregating that knowledge outweighs the benefits of doing so.

Try as he might, Mises could not exempt the capitalist corporation from the problem of bureaucracy. One cannot define bureaucracy out of existence, or overcome the problem of distributed knowledge, simply by using the word "entrepreneur." Mises tried to make the bureaucratic or nonbureaucratic character of an organization a simple matter of its organizational goals rather than its functioning. The motivation of the corporate employee, from the CEO down to the production worker, by definition, will be profit-seeking; his will is in harmony with that of the stockholder because he belongs to the stockholder's organization.

By defining organizational goals as "profit-seeking," Mises – like the neoclassicals – treated the internal workings of the organization as a black box. In treating the internal policies of the capitalist corporation as inherently profit-driven, Mises simultaneously treated the entrepreneur as an indivisible actor whose will and perception permeate the entire organization. Mises's entrepreneur was a brooding omnipresence, guiding the actions of every employee from CEO to janitor.

He viewed the separation of ownership from control, and the knowledge and agency problems resulting from it, as largely nonexistent. The invention of double-entry bookkeeping, which made possible the separate calculation of profit and loss in each division of an enterprise, has "reliev[ed] the entrepreneur of involvement in too much detail," Mises writes in Human Action. The only thing necessary to transform every single employee of a corporation, from CEO on down, into a perfect instrument of his will was the ability to monitor the balance sheet of any division or office and fire the functionary responsible for red ink. Mises continues:

> It is the system of double-entry bookkeeping that makes the functioning of the managerial system possible. Thanks to it, the entrepreneur is in a position to separate the calculation of each part of his total enterprise in such a way that he can determine the role it plays within his whole enterprise. . . . Within this system of business calculation each section of a firm represents an integral entity, a hypothetical independent business, as it were. It is assumed that this section "owns" a definite part of the whole capital employed in the enterprise, that it buys from other sections and sells to them, that it has its own expenses and its own revenues, that its dealings result either in a profit or in a loss which is imputed to its own conduct of affairs as distinguished from the result of the other sections. Thus the entrepreneur can assign to each section's management a great deal of independence. The only directive he gives to a man whom he entrusts with the management of a circumscribed job is to make as much profit as possible. An examination of the accounts shows how

successful or unsuccessful the managers were in executing this directive. Every manager and submanager is responsible for the working of his section or subsection. . . . His own interests impel him toward the utmost care and exertion in the conduct of his section's affairs. If he incurs losses, he will be replaced by a man whom the entrepreneur expects to be more successful, or the whole section will be discontinued.

Capital Markets as Control Mechanism

Mises also identified outside capital markets as a control mechanism limiting managerial discretion. Of the popular conception of stockholders as passive rentiers in the face of managerial control, he wrote:

> This doctrine disregards entirely the role that the capital and money market, the stock and bond exchange, which a pertinent idiom simply calls the "market," plays in the direction of corporate business. . . . In fact, the changes in the prices of . . . stock and of corporate bonds are the means applied by the capitalists for the supreme control of the flow of capital. The price structure as determined by the speculations on the capital and money markets and on the big commodity exchanges not only decides how much capital is available for the conduct of each corporation's business; it creates a state of affairs to which the managers must adjust their operations in detail.

One can hardly imagine the most hubristic of state socialist central planners taking a more optimistic view of the utopian potential of numbers-crunching.

Peter Klein argued that this foreshadowed Henry Manne's treatment of the mechanism by which entrepreneurs maintain control of corporate management. So long as there is a market for control of corporations, the discretion of management will be limited by the threat of hostile takeover. Although management possesses a fair degree of administrative autonomy, any significant deviation from profit-maximization will lower stock prices and bring the corporation into danger of outside takeover.

The question, though, is whether those making investment decisions – whether senior management allocating capital among divisions of a corporation or outside finance capitalists – even possess the information needed to assess the internal workings of firms and make appropriate decisions.

How far the real-world, state capitalist allocation of finance differs from Mises's picture is suggested by Robert Jackall's account in *Moral Mazes* of the internal workings of a corporation (especially the notorious practices of "starving," or "milking," an organization in order to inflate its apparent short-term profit). Whether an apparent profit is sustainable, or an illusory side effect of eating the seed corn, is often a judgment best made by those directly involved in production. The purely money calculations of those at the top do not suffice for a valid assessment of such questions.

One big problem with Mises's model of entrepreneurial central planning by double-entry bookkeeping is this: it is often the irrational constraints imposed from above that result in red ink at lower levels. But those at the top of the hierarchy refuse to acknowledge the double bind they put their subordinates in. "Plausible deniability," the downward flow of responsibility and upward flow of credit, and the practice of shooting the messenger for bad news, are what lubricate the wheels of any large organization.

As for outside investors, participants in the capital markets are even further removed than management from the data needed to evaluate the efficiency of factor use within the "black box." In practice, hostile takeovers tend to gravitate toward firms with low debt loads and apparently low short-term profit margins. The corporate raiders are more likely to smell blood when there is the possibility of loading up an acquisition with new debt and stripping it of assets for short-term returns. The best way to avoid a hostile takeover, on the other hand, is to load an organization with debt and inflate the short-term returns by milking. Another problem, from the perspective of those at the top, is determining the significance of red or black ink. How does the large-scale investor distinguish losses caused by senior management's gaming of the system in its own interest at the expense of the productivity of the organization from losses occurring as normal effects of the business cycle? Mises of all people, who rejected the neoclassicals' econometric approach precisely because the variables were too complex to control for, should have anticipated such difficulties.

Management's "gaming" might well be a purely defensive response to structural incentives, a way of deflecting pressure from those above whose only concern is to maximize apparent profits without regard to how short-term savings might result in long-term loss. The practices of "starving" and "milking" organizations that Jackall made so much of—deferring needed maintenance costs, letting plant and equipment run down, and the like, in order to inflate the quarterly balance sheet—resulted from just such pressure, as irrational as the pressures Soviet enterprise managers faced from Gosplan.

Shared Culture

The problem is complicated when the same organizational culture—determined by the needs of the managerial system itself—is shared by all the corporations in a state-induced oligopoly industry, so that the same pattern of red ink appears industry-wide. It's complicated still further when the general atmosphere of state capitalism enables the corporations in a cartelized industry to operate in the black despite excessive size and dysfunctional internal culture. It becomes impossible to make a valid assessment of why the corporation is profitable at all: does the black ink result from efficiency or from some degree of protection against the competitive penalty for inefficiency? If the decisions of MBA types to engage in asset-stripping and milking, in the interest of short-term profitability, result in long-term harm to the health of the enterprise, they are more apt to be reinforced than censured by investors and higher-ups. After all, they acted according to the conventional wisdom in the Big MBA Handbook, so it couldn't have been that that caused them to go in the tank. Must've been sunspots or something.

In fact, the financial community sometimes censures transgressions against the norms of corporate culture even when they are quite successful by conventional measures. Costco's stock fell in value, despite the company's having outperformed Wal-Mart in profit, in response to adverse publicity in the business community about its above-average wages. Deutsche Bank analyst Bill Dreher snidely remarked,

"At Costco, it's better to be an employee or a customer than a shareholder." Nevertheless, in the world of faith-based investment, Wal-Mart "remains the darling of the Street, which, like Wal-Mart and many other companies, believes that shareholders are best served if employers do all they can to hold down costs, including the cost of labor" (*Business Week Online*, April 12, 2004).

On the other hand, management may be handsomely rewarded for running a corporation into the ground, so long as it is perceived to be doing everything right according to the norms of corporate culture. In a New York Times story that Digg aptly titled "Home Depot CEO Gets $210M Severance for Sucking at Job," it was reported that departing Home Depot CEO Robert Nardelli received an enormous severance package despite abysmal performance. It's a good thing he didn't raise employee wages too high, though, or he'd be eating in a soup kitchen.

As you might expect, the usual suspects stepped in to defend Nardelli's honor. An Allan Murray article at the *Wall Street Journal* noted that he had "more than doubled . . . earnings."

But Tom Blumor of BizzyBlog, whose sources for obvious reasons prefer to remain anonymous, pointed out some inconvenient facts about how Nardelli achieved those increased earnings:

- His consolidation of purchasing and many other functions to Atlanta from several regions caused buyers to lose touch with their vendors . . . .

- Firing knowledgeable and experienced people in favor of uninformed newbies and part-timers greatly reduced payroll and benefits costs, but has eventually driven customers away, and given the company a richly-deserved reputation for mediocre service . . . .

- Nardelli and his minions played every accounting, acquisition, and quick-fix angle they could to keep the numbers looking good, while letting the business deteriorate.

In a follow-up comment directed to me personally, Blumer provided this additional bit of information:

> I have since learned that Nardelli, in the last months before he walked, took the entire purchasing function out of Atlanta and moved it to . . . India – Of all the things to pick for foreign outsourcing.
>
> I am told that "out of touch" doesn't even begin to describe how bad it is now between HD stores and Purchasing, and between HD Purchasing and suppliers. Not only is there a language dialect barrier, but the purchasing people in India don't know the "language" of American hardware – or even what half the stuff the stores and suppliers are describing even is.
>
> I am told that an incredible amount of time, money, and energy is being wasted – all in the name of what was in all likelihood a bonus-driven goal for cutting headcount and making G&A [general and administrative] expenses look low ("look" low because the expenses have been pushed down to the stores and suppliers).

More than one observer has remarked on the similarity, in their distorting effects, of the incentives within the Soviet state-planning system and the Western corporate economy. We already noted the systemic pressure to create the illusion of short-term profit by undermining long-term productivity.

Consider Hayek's prediction of the uneven development, irrationality, and misallocation of resources within a planned economy ("Socialist Calculation II: The State of the Debate"):

> There is no reason to expect that production would stop, or that the authorities would find difficulty in using all the available resources somehow, or even that output would be permanently lower than it had been before planning started . . . . [We should expect] the excessive development of some lines of production at the expense of others and the use of methods which are inappropriate under the circumstances. We should expect to find overdevelopment of some industries at a cost which was not justified by the importance of their increased output and see unchecked the ambition of the engineer to apply the latest development elsewhere, without considering whether they were economically suited in the situation. In many cases the use of the latest methods of production, which could not have been applied without central planning, would then be a symptom of a misuse of resources rather than a proof of success.

As an example he cited "the excellence, from a technological point of view, of some parts of the Russian industrial equipment, which often strikes the casual observer and which is commonly regarded as evidence of success."

To anyone observing the uneven development of the corporate economy under state capitalism, this should inspire a sense of déjà vu. Entire categories of goods and production methods have been developed at enormous expense, either within military industry or by state-subsidized R&D in the civilian economy, without regard to cost. Subsidies to capital accumulation, R&D, and technical education radically distort the forms taken by production. (On these points see David Noble's works, *Forces of Production* and *America by Design.*) Blockbuster factories and economic centralization become artificially profitable, thanks to the Interstate Highway system and other means of externalizing distribution costs.

Pervasive Irrationality

It also describes quite well the environment of pervasive irrationality within the large corporation: management featherbedding and self-dealing; "cost-cutting" measures that decimate productive resources while leaving management's petty empires intact; and the tendency to extend bureaucratic domain while cutting maintenance and support for existing obligations. Management's allocation of resources no doubt creates use value of a sort – but with no reliable way to assess opportunity cost or determine whether the benefit was worth it.

A good example is a hospital, part of a corporate chain, that I've had occasion to observe first-hand. Management justifies repeated downsizings of nurses and technicians as "cost-cutting" measures despite increased costs from errors, falls, and MRSA (Methicillin-resistant Staphylococcus aureus) infections that exceed the alleged savings. Of course the "cost-cutting" justification for downsizing direct caregivers doesn't extend to the patronage network of staff RNs attached to the Nursing Office. Meanwhile, management pours money into ill-considered capital projects (like remodeling jobs that actually make wards less functional, or the extremely expensive new ACE unit that never opened because it was so badly designed); an expensive surgical robot, purchased mainly for prestige value, does nothing that couldn't be accomplished by scrubbing in an extra nurse. But the management team is hardly likely to face any negative consequences, when the region's three other large hospitals are run exactly the same way.

Such pathologies, obviously, are not the result of the free market. That is not to say, of course, that bigness as such would not produce inefficiency costs in some firms that might exist under laissez faire. The calculation problem (in the broad sense that includes Hayekian information problems) may or may not exist to some extent in the private corporation in a free market. But the boundary between market and hierarchy would be set by the point at which the benefits of size cease to outweigh the costs of such calculation problems. The inefficiencies of large size and hierarchy may be a matter of degree, but, as Ronald Coase said, the market would determine whether the inefficiencies are worth it.

The problem is that the state, by artificially reducing the costs of large size and restraining the competitive ill effects of calculation problems, promotes larger size than would be the case in a free market – and with it calculation problems to a pathological extent. The state promotes inefficiencies of large size and hierarchy past the point at which they cease to be worth it, from a standpoint of net social efficiency, because those receiving the benefits of large size are not the same parties who pay the costs of inefficiency.

The solution is to eliminate the state policies that have created the situation, and allow the market to punish inefficiency. To get there, though, some libertarians need to reexamine their unquestioned sympathies for big business as an "oppressed minority" and remember that they're supposed to be defending free markets – not the winners under the current statist economy.

CHAPTER

SIX

WHY CORPORATE CAPITALISM IS UNSUSTAINABLE

KEVIN CARSON

I'm not a Marxist, but I find a lot of Marx's ideas useful. Old Karl certainly had a gift for turning a phrase. Nobody who could come up with something as Proudhonian as "the associated producers" could be all bad. One of his best in my opinion was that new productive forces eventually "become incompatible with their capitalist integument," at which point "the integument is burst asunder."

Another source of vivid imagery is the Preamble to the Constitution of the Industrial Workers of the World. Consider this: "... we are forming the structure of the new society within the shell of the old."

These two phrases brilliantly describe the predicament of state-fostered corporate capitalism. Capitalism as an

https://c4ss.org/content/10498

historic system is five hundred or more years old, and the state was intimately involved in its formation and its ongoing preservation from the very beginning. But the state has been far more involved, if such a thing is possible, in the model of corporate capitalism that's prevailed over the past 150 years. The corporate titans that dominate our economic and political life could hardly survive for a year without the continuing intervention of the state in the market to sustain them through subsidies and monopoly protections.

This system is reaching its limits of sustainability. Here are some reasons why:

1. The monopolies on which it depends are increasingly unenforceable. Especially "intellectual property."
   (a) Copyright-based industry has already lost the fight to end file-sharing.
   (b) Industrial patents are only enforceable when oligopoly industry, oligopoly retail chains reduce transaction cost of enforcement — unenforceable against neighborhood garage factories using pirated CAD/CAM files.
2. Cheap production tools and soil-efficient horticulture are
   (a) increasing competition from self-employment
   (b) reducing profitable investment opportunities for surplus capital and destroying direct rate of profit (DROP)
3. State-subsidized production inputs leads to geometrically increasing demand for those inputs, outstripping

the state's ability to supply and driving it into chronic fiscal crisis. For centuries the state has provided large-scale capitalist agribusiness with privileged access to land stolen from the laboring classes. For 150 years, it has subsidized inputs like railroads, airports and highways for long-distance shipping, and irrigation water for factory farming. But as any student of Microecon 101 could tell you, subsidizing something means more and more of it gets consumed. So you get agribusiness that's inefficient in its use of land and water, and industry that achieves false economies of scale by producing for artificially large market areas. Each year it takes a larger government subsidy to keep this business model profitable.

4. Worsening tendencies toward overaccumulation and stagnation increase the amount of chronic deficit spending necessary for Keynesian aggregate demand management, also worsening the fiscal crisis. The state has built a massive military-industrial complex and created entire other industries at state expense to absorb excess investment capital and overcome the system's tendency toward surplus production and surplus capital, and sustained larger and larger deficits, just to prevent the collapse that otherwise would have already occurred.

In short, capitalism depends on ever-growing amounts of state intervention in the market for its survival, and the system is hitting the point where the teat runs dry. The result is a system in which governments and corporations are increasingly hollowed out. And meanwhile, growing up within this corporate capitalist "integument," things like open source software and culture, open-source industrial design, permaculture and low-overhead garage micromanufacturing eat the corporate-state economy alive. An ever-growing share of labor and production are disappearing into relocalized resilient economies, self-employment, worker cooperatives and the informal and household economy. In the end, they will skeletonize the corporate dinosaurs like a swarm of piranha.

CHAPTER

SEVEN

ENGAGEMENT WITH THE LEFT ON FREE MARKETS

KEVIN CARSON

A very provocative discussion, provoked by Chris Sciabarra's post at *Liberty & Power.*[1]

Anthony Gregory first commented:

> If libertarians can explain that the right actually opposes free markets, but instead embraces corporatism and state capitalism, the battle to win them over will be half-won. One reason they don't like markets is because people like Bush pretend to like them, but I think the left is catching on.

Jeanine Ring added that much of the Left's problem with corporate capitalism is cultural: an "antagonism to corpo-

https://c4ss.org/content/15576

[1]http://hnn.us/blogs/4.html

rations into just mercantilist exploration but the heirarchical, conformist structure and "Dilbert" culture of corporate modernity." She goes on

> If libertarians favor a world where corporations aren't the specially priviledged, legally impersoned default forms of social organization, they should some thoughts as to what 'human scale' forms of socio-commercial relations might look like.

Sciabarra responded, however, that most radical leftists see the corporate system as an inevitable outgrowth of the free market.

> They, like many libertarians, have argued that the state has always been intimately involved in markets, acting on behalf of those who are most adept at using political power. For Marxists and other radical left-wingers, however, this means that political power is systematically skewed in favor of business interests. The ideology of free-markets is, therefore, a mere apologia for a class-biased reality that is inescapable as long as private property and market exchange exist.

It follows, he said, that "until or unless libertarians can convince the left that there is an 'unknown ideal' to free markets, that corporatism is not an inevitability, I doubt that there will be any lasting peace with the left."

So it seems that any attempt by the anti-corporatist free market movement to engage with the mainstream Left will focus, of necessity, on a few issues. First is a rehabilitation of the term "free market" itself to mean more than the cash nexus, encompassing rather the entire sphere of voluntary non-coercive social relations. As Karl Hess pointed out over thirty years ago, the free market movement is (or should be) a people's movement. Any "free market" ideology that has no room for the commons as a form of "private property," for workers' and consumers' co-ops, or for hippie dippy stuff like Hess' own "community technology" experiments in the Adams-Morgan Organization, is no "free market" ideology that I want to be a part of (apologies to Rosa Luxembourg).

Second item on the agenda is getting right with Robert Anton Wilson. That is: to identify the free market with the system of voluntary exchange of labor between producers that remains when the state no longer intervenes on behalf of privileged classes. It would help mightily if the Left could see the free market as a residuum of voluntary relations that persists in any society, in the interstices of state power, and exists in potentia as the basis of a new society when state-enforced class domination is abolished. The libertarian Left is fond of the Wobbly slogan, "Building the structure of the new society within the shell of the old." So they are already familiar with the idea that the seeds of a free society exist within the present system, and can gradually supplant the system of class privilege as the state is rolled back. The Left is already amenable to Gustav Landauer's "condition, a certain relationship among human beings, a mode of behavior" with which to supplant the state; and Paul Goodman's "spheres of free action." We just need to do a better job of expressing our free market vision in similar terms.

If the market and the state have coexisted historically, they can be separated logically. The question of whether class differences originally arose from successful competition in the market, and the state was then called in to reinforce the position of the winners; or whether the class differences first arose from state interference, is a vital one. The fact that the state has been intertwined with every "actually existing" *market* in history is beside the point; social anarchists themselves face a similar challenge — that the state has been intertwined with every *society* in history. The response, in both cases, is essentially the same — the seeds of a non-exploitative order exist within every system of exploitation.

Our goal, not only as anarchists but as free market anarchists, is to supplant the state with voluntary relations. If the absence of something in historical times, in a society based on division of labor, is a damning challenge — well then, they're damned as well as we are.

The questions of whether state capitalism is an inevitable outgrowth of the free market, of whether decentralized and libertarian forms of industrial production can exist under worker control in a market society, etc., are at least questions on which we can approach the Left with logic and evidence. They are, for the most part, rational and open to persuasion. At the very least, there is room for constructive engagement. And remember, it is not an all-or-nothing matter. It is possible, if nothing else, to reduce the area of disagreement on a case-by-case basis.

CHAPTER

EIGHT

SIX THESES OF LIBERTARIAN RHETORIC

RODERICK T. LONG

In *The Structure of Scientific Revolutions*[1] (a book of great virtues and great flaws, but I'm not going to get into either right now), Thomas Kuhn describes an experiment that I think is of tremendous importance to libertarians, particularly left-libertarians:

> In a psychological experiment that deserves to be far better known outside the trade, Bruner and Postman [1949] asked experimental subjects to identify on short and controlled exposure a series of playing cards. Many of the cards were normal, but some were made anomalous, e.g., a red six of spades and

http://c4ss.org/content/35964

[1]http://www.amazon.com/Structure-Scientific-Revolutions-Thomas-Kuhn/dp/0226458083/praxeologynet-20

a black four of hearts. Each experimental run was constituted by the display of a single card to a single subject in a series of gradually increased exposures. After each exposure the subject was asked what he had seen, and the run was terminated by two successive correct identifications.

Even on the shortest exposures many subjects identified most of the cards, and after a small increase all the subjects identified them all. For the normal cards these identifications were usually correct, but the anomalous cards were almost always identified, without apparent hesitation or puzzlement, as normal. The black four of hearts might, for example, be identified as the four of either spades or hearts. Without any awareness of trouble, it was immediately fitted to one of the conceptual categories prepared by prior experience. One would not even like to say that the subjects had seen something different from what they had identified.

With a further increase of exposure to the anomalous cards, subjects did begin to hesitate and to display awareness of anomaly. Exposed, for example to the red six of spades, some would say: That's the six of spades, but there's something wrong with it – the black has a red border. Further increase of exposure resulted in still more hesitation and confusion until finally, and sometimes quite suddenly, most subjects would produce the correct identification without hesitation. Moreover, after doing this with two or three of the anomalous cards, they would have little further difficulty with the others.

> A few subjects, however, were never able to make the requisite adjustment of their categories. Even at forty times the average exposure required to recognize normal cards for what they were, more than 10% of the anomalous cards were not correctly identified. And the subjects who then failed often experienced acute personal distress. One of them exclaimed: 'I can't make the suit out, whatever it is. It didn't even look like a card that time. I don't know what color it is now or whether it's a spade or a heart. I'm not even sure now what a spade looks like. My God!' ... My colleague Postman tells me that, though knowing all about the apparatus and display in advance, he nevertheless found looking at the incongruous cards acutely uncomfortable.

In short, people have enormous difficulty with, and often a strong aversion to, recognising something that doesn't fit their established categories. And this helps, I think, to explain why as libertarians, and in particular as left-libertarians, we have so much trouble getting our message across; for in the mainstream political realm we are black hearts and red spades. Most people's first impulse is to assimilate us to some familiar category – and since we talk so much about the virtues of free markets and the evils of government, we tend to get lumped with conservatives, since they make similar noises. When more prolonged exposure persuades people that we're not quite conservatives after all, they then tend to become convinced that we're black spades with red borders — conventionally conservative on some issues, conventionally liberal on others (a tendency we ourselves encourage with our in part useful, in part misleading Nolan Charts[2]) — as opposed to representing a radical alternative to existing ideologies.

The moral, I think, is that libertarians, and especially left-libertarians, need to focus more on simply getting our position recognised. Getting it recognised is of course not enough — one then has to *argue* that the position is *correct* – but I think such argument and defense are to a large extent pointless if people can't see what the position being defended even *is*.

Our vital task, then, is to get the word out that there *is* a position out there that includes the following theses:

1. Big business and big government are (for the most part) natural allies.

2. Although conservative politicians pretend to hate big government, and liberal politicians pretend to hate big business, most mainstream policies — *both* liberal and conservative — involve (slightly different versions of) massive intervention on behalf of the big-business/big-government elite at the expense of ordinary people.

3. Liberal politicians cloak their intervention on behalf of the strong in the rhetoric of intervention on behalf of the weak; conservative politicians cloak their intervention on behalf of the strong in the rhetoric of non-intervention and free markets – but in both cases the rhetoric is belied by the reality.

4. A genuine policy of intervention on behalf of the weak, if liberals actually tried it, wouldn't work either, since

[2]http://en.wikipedia.org/wiki/Nolan_Chart

the nature of government power would automatically warp it toward the interests of the elite.

5. A genuine policy of non-intervention and free markets, if conservatives actually tried it, *would* work, since free competition would empower ordinary people at the expense of the elite.

6. Since conservative policies, despite their associated free-market rhetoric, are mostly the diametrical opposite of free-market policies, the failures of conservative policies do not constitute an objection to (but rather, if anything, a vindication of) free-market policies.

Of course we should be prepared to *defend* these theses through economic reasoning and historical evidence, but the main goal at this point, I think, should be not so much to defend them as simply to advertise their existence. We need to make our red spades and black hearts a sufficiently familiar feature of the intellectual landscape that people will be able to see them for what they are rather than misclassifying them – at which point we'll be in a better position to defend them. (Though admittedly point 6 is already beginning to slide from description to defense; still, I think 6 is crucial to getting our position so much as a hearing.)

What I advocate, then, is to make the constant repetition of (some equivalent of) points 1 through 6 a constant feature of our propagandising. In conversation, in articles, in letters to the editor, we should hit points 1 through 6 over and over again. The cure for resistance to the unfamiliar is to make it familiar.

CHAPTER

NINE

THE RETURN OF LEVIATHAN: CAN WE PREVENT IT?

RODERICK T. LONG

The Three Leviathans

Two years ago, at our Spring 1994 Forum on Systems of Law, I suggested that those seeking to build and maintain a Free Nation would face three problems, which I called "the three Leviathans":

> Leviathan Past (that is, the dangers posed by the state presently occupying the territory within which the Free Nation is to arise), Leviathan Present (that is, the dangers posed, once the Free Nation has arisen, by the threat of other states existing outside the Free Nation's territory), and Leviathan Yet to

https://c4ss.org/content/21105

> Come (that is, the dangers posed by the unwanted but all-too-possible emergence of a state within the Free Nation's territory — that is, the possible evolution of the ... Free Nation into a [statist régime].[1]

With regard to Leviathan Past, I noted that there are two ways of getting an existing régime to give up its power and turn libertarian: force and persuasion. Arguing that force was impractical, I suggested three possible modes of persuasion: a) convert the rulers of a country to libertarianism (a daunting prospect); b) convert the ordinary citizens to libertarianism and get them to vote in a libertarian system; and c) pay the rulers to relinquish sovereignty over some portion of their territory. More recently, I have returned to the topic of Leviathan Past, and argued that the vestiges of the old régime in a fledgling libertarian society might be successfully bought off and so discouraged from engaging in obstructionism.[2]

With regard to Leviathan Present, I have since argued that this threat can be met through a combination of voluntary contributions and for-profit defense agencies.[3,4]

What about Leviathan Yet to Come? In my initial Forum presentation I argued that this threat was minimal. My argument relied on traditional libertarian class analysis, which

---

[1]Roderick T. Long, "Implementing Private Law in a World of States," *Proceedings of a Forum on the Subject: Systems of Law* (30 April 1994).

[2]Roderick T. Long, "Dismantling Leviathan From Within, Part IV: The Sons of Brutus," elsewhere in the present issue.

[3]Roderick T. Long, "Funding Public Goods: Six Solutions," in *Formulations*, Vol. II, No. 1 (Autumn 1994).

[4]Roderick T. Long, "Defending a Free Nation," in *Formulations*, Vol. II, No. 2 (Winter 1994-95).

maintains that a ruling class cannot achieve or maintain power except through the mechanism of the state. Thus a ruling class is the product of governmental institutions and not vice versa.

More recently, however, I have rethought this point. In fact, ruling classes have managed throughout human history to survive and dominate even in stateless or near-stateless societies, through a combination of economic patronage and religious status.[5] A state may dramatically increase the power of a ruling class, but it is not an absolute prerequisite for the existence of such a class. Still, I've argued, there are reasons for optimism: modern society cannot sustain the kind of religious climate needed for the moral support of a ruling class,[6,7] and a genuine free market would eliminate the kind of economic dependence that makes people vulnerable to intimidation by the wealthy.[8,9] I've also argued that attempts by some groups to form cooperative schemes to oppress other groups are likely to backfire in a completely free market.[10]

So there are reasons for optimism. But there are also reasons for caution. We know from history that the Leviathan

[5]Roderick T. Long, "Can We Escape the Ruling Class?," in *Formulations*, Vol. II, No. 1 (Autumn 1994).

[6]*Ibid.*

[7]Roderick T. Long, "Religious Influence on Political Structure: Lessons from the Past, Prospects for the Future," in *Formulations*, Vol. II, No. 3 (Spring 1995).

[8]Roderick T. Long, "Who's the Scrooge? Libertarians and Compassion," in *Formulations*, Vol. I, No. 2 (Winter 1993-94).

[9]Roderick T. Long, letters exchange with Kevin Whiteacre, "Our Readers Write," in *Formulations*, Vol. III, No. 2 (Winter 1995-96).

[10]Roderick T. Long, "Good and Bad Collective Action: Can We Nourish One and Squelch the Other?," in *Formulations*, Vol. III, No. 1 (Autumn 1995).

virus is a robust one. If it finds a niche, it will cling, and grow. Eternal vigilance is the price of liberty. It is appropriate, then, for those who seek to build a Free Nation to return again and again to the question of how to stay free.

Why Do People Want Leviathan?

Statist régimes exist because people want them. This is not to say that such régimes arise, and maintain themselves in existence, solely through the deliberate choices of individuals. On the contrary, the growth of government is often a spontaneous and quite unintended side effect of human actions pursuing quite different goals. Nevertheless, if the result were entirely unwelcome I do not think it would long survive. Why, then, do people so often desire a powerful coercive state?

There are any number of reasons, of course. Let me mention just four: two reasons that depend on intellectual mistakes, and another two that depend on more intractable facts about human psychology.

One intellectual mistake is the idea that certain desirable goals can be achieved only through coercive authority. Those on the left do not see how people could be protected from poverty, pollution, or discrimination except through the benevolent arm of the state; likewise, those on the right see governmental intervention as a prerequisite for the preservation of moral and cultural values. People who actually lived in a Free Nation, however, would see these benefits being provided without any government involvement; so this intellectual mistake would be less likely to occur, once freedom was achieved.

A second intellectual mistake underlying statism is bit more slippery, however. Statists generally think that one's willingness to *enforce* a moral claim is a mark of the importance one attaches to that claim. Even if a free-market system does an excellent job of supplying food to the poor, the fact that such a system does not recognize any *right* to be fed shows its insensitivity to the importance of hunger relief. When libertarians claim that we have a right to drive a motorcycle without a helmet, but no right to be protected from starvation or discrimination, the statists conclude (not without justification, in the case of *some* libertarians!) that libertarians regard freedom from helmets as *more important* than freedom from starvation or discrimination. And so the statists, reasonably enough given their premises, dismiss the libertarian position as absurd.

This motivation for statism would not necessarily vanish simply as a result of the statists' seeing that the needs they regard as important are indeed met in a Free Nation. They would still insist that the importance of these needs be underscored by having their provision enforced by an agency speaking for the community as a whole. (Even libertarians have been known to succumb to this sort of reasoning; for example, it was on the basis of considerations rather like these that Robert Nozick was led, in *The Examined Life*, to repudiate the libertarian position he had defended in *Anarchy, State, and Utopia.*)[11]

The only cure for this mistake is education. The statist must be brought to see that the libertarian position on the use of force is based on reciprocity, not on assessments of

[11]Robert Nozick, "The Zigzag of Politics"; in *The Examined Life: Philosophical Meditations* (New York: Simon & Schuster, 1989).

importance. Evils involving force may legitimately be fought by means of force; evils not involving force must be fought by other means. (It would certainly help matters if libertarians themselves would refrain from speaking as though coercion were a *more serious* evil than any other. Stealing a grape is an act of force, persistent emotional and psychological abuse is not, but the latter is a far greater evil than the former.) To some extent, though, this second mistake is supported by the first, in that statists may find the libertarian position more plausible when they come to recognize that there *are* effective non-coercive ways of fighting evils.

But the hankering after Leviathan also rests on two psychological factors that cannot be so easily eradicated: the desire to control, and the desire to be controlled.

The desire to control can take the form of a love of power for power's own sake. But it needn't. People also seek power as a means to other ends. Whenever we seek some goal that requires the cooperation of others, and those others refuse to cooperate, there is an opening for the temptation to *force* them to cooperate. And when many people succumb to the temptation to compel the cooperation of many other people, we are well on our way to statism. This is probably a permanent aspect of the human condition. The best we can do is:

(a) provide a moral climate in which this temptation will be easy to resist, by teaching people to regard it as shameful and ignoble to live by violence rather than persuasion;

(b) point out, as well, that any attempt to establish a state is likely to backfire, as people with aims other than one's own may end up holding the reins of power; and

(c) for those who prove impervious to moral suasion and politico-economic analysis alike, make it clear to such people that their attempts to control others will not be tolerated.

The desire to govern is easy enough to understand, to the extent that it is the byproduct of a more general desire to see one's ends fulfilled. The desire to be governed is more puzzling. How could such a desire arise?

I suspect that the desire to be governed is the result of an evolutionary trade-off. Animals at the bottom of the evolutionary ladder (insects, fish, and the like) operate almost entirely on instinct. Very little of their behavior is learned; for the most part it is encoded in their genes, and passed from one generation to another through biological reproduction. As we pass to more advanced species, however, we find the ratio of learned to instinctual behavior steadily increasing, until we reach human beings, whose ability to learn is tremendous — and whose repertoire of instinctive behavior is minimal.

Reliance on learning rather than instinct makes for a more flexible and versatile organism; when environmental conditions change, animals whose behavior is not pre-programmed can adapt more quickly. Moreover, animals with the capacity to learn can acquire new, successful behavioral strategies by imitating one another. They do not have to wait for a random mutation in order to acquire the new behavior; and in addition, knowledge can now be transmitted to all the other members of one's species, not solely one's immediate descendants; cultural reproduction is thus more efficient than biological reproduction. Species that rely heavily on instinct, by contrast, are less flexible, and so rely on quantity rather than quality in their reproductive strategies; rather than raising just one or two offspring and investing time and effort teaching them the skills needed to survive, as occurs in the higher animals, the lower animals produce hundreds of offspring at once, and turn them loose with little or no guidance.

So we're lucky to be human. Hooray for us. There is a downside to all this, though. Because we depend so heavily on learning and are so ill-equipped with instincts, it takes us a long time to acquire the ability to survive on our own. Many insects begin life entirely alone, with the parents long since dead or flown off; the insect knows instinctually how to go about surviving. As we climb the evolutionary ladder, dependence on parenting increases; but even here we find, e.g., that colts can stand and walk, albeit shakily, from the day they are born. Human beings, because of our heavy learning-to-instinct ratio — that ratio that is our glory, that makes us what we are — also have the longest childhoods, the longest period of dependence. Thus we (master learners that we are) learn early that we need someone to take care of us, to make our decisions for us. And what we learn earliest is the most deeply ingrained, the most difficult to unlearn. Hence the desire for the State, as a replacement for the Parent.

So human beings have, all too often, a desire to be controlled. Fortunately, we also have a desire *not* to be controlled, a desire to make our own decisions; and this desire manifests itself very early as well. These two desires conflict, and circumstances may influence the outcome of the conflict. Here too, then, a crucial role of education is to reinforce our libertarian impulses and to discourage our statist impulses. (And to the extent that the desire to be controlled cannot be suppressed, perhaps it can be channeled into less destructive manifestations; e.g., this desire might be satisfied by joining a religious cult rather than setting up a powerful government.)

As for the intellectual mistakes that support the yearning for Leviathan, perhaps the most important task for educators in a Free Nation (whether parents, teachers, or what have you) is to help people learn how to think straight. I recently had an opportunity to reread the Constitution of North Carolina, and I was struck by the difference, not so much in content as in *language*, between the original 18th-century provisions and the more recent amendments. (As in most state constitutions, the original wording and the later amendments are all jumbled together, rather than clearly differentiated as they are in the U.S. Constitution. Still, it's easy enough to distinguish the earlier parts from the later ones.) The founders of the United Sates, men of the 18th-century Enlightenment, used words with a grace and precision rarely met with today (and least of all in today's politicians!). They took language *seriously*. They wrote clearly, carefully, incisively. When they set down a sentence, they meant something definite by it, not some vague mush. By contrast, the more recent provisions are full of inanities like "everyone shall have a right to the privilege of education" — a sure sign that the writers are navigating the hallways of thought by touch, not by sight.

Television is often blamed for having shortened people's attention spans and their ability to deal with complex issues;

but there is nothing inherent in the nature of television as a medium that requires such a result. Rather, I think public education is the primary culprit here, for making such a boring and painful process out of reading, writing, and thinking that all too often the student's intellectual muscles are crippled, his curiosity deadened, his pilot light effectively snuffed out.

The case for libertarianism is complicated. It rests on very broad generalizations, drawn from history and theory alike. It requires a capacity to think in principled terms, be the principles moral or economic. If the citizens of a Free Nation do not understand the case for liberty, they will not support it. Thus, a libertarian society cannot hope to survive unless the educational system is radically transformed. (I hope to return to this subject in a future article.)

Libertarian Structures

So far I've been talking about how to maintain freedom in "a" libertarian society. But of course there are different possible models for a libertarian society, with different political and legal structures, and the threat from Leviathan Yet to Come may take rather different forms, and so require correspondingly different measures, in libertarian societies differing in structure.

There seem to me to be three main varieties of libertarian structure: the constitutionalist model, the proprietary model, and the pure market model. (There are also subvarieties of each of these.) Do these structures differ at all in their susceptibility to the Leviathan virus?

The Constitutionalist Model

Under the constitutionalist model, a single agency is charged with protecting libertarian rights within a given territory; this agency is then designed in such a way as to make it as difficult as possible for it to transform itself into Leviathan.

The constitutionalist model comes in both minarchist and quasi-anarchist varieties. In the minarchist version, the single agency holds a coercive monopoly over legal services within the territory; no competitors are permitted. In the quasi-anarchist version, competitors are not prohibited, and a few may function around the edges, but the dominant agency nevertheless holds a monopoly or near-monopoly, not through any coercion on its part, but because other nations regard it as the legitimate government and will deal only with it, so that it becomes more important for residents of the Free Nation to influence that agency's policies than to influence the policies of rival agencies. (The dominant agency may, for example, be the holder of a 99-year lease of sovereignty on the Free Nation's territory.)

A constitutionalist model is extremely risky. Nothing is better positioned to transform itself into Leviathan than a government (or quasi-government), however minimal. Being the dominant provider of protective services has been a stepping-stone to governmental power many times in history. In ancient times, that's how Rome and Athens acquired their empires; in mediæval times, that's how Aelfred King of Wessex became Aelfred King of England.

But the constitutionalist model has its advantages as well. While it may be highly susceptible to the virus of Leviathan

Yet to Come, it is perhaps the most impervious to the viruses of Leviathans Past and Present. A libertarian society that can turn a governmental face toward the outside world, that *looks* to other nations like a state and can negotiate *as* a state, is more likely to be taken seriously and treated with respect in the community of nations. By contrast, if it looks to outsiders as though "nobody is in charge," hostile powers may take this as an invitation to invade in order to "restore order," and world opinion will put up little protest.

Suppose we do opt for the constitutionalist model; how should we design our minimal state (if we go the minarchist route) or our dominant protection agency (if we go the quasi-anarchist route) so as to minimize the likelihood that it will grow and seize power? This is a topic I've addressed in a number of earlier articles,[12,13,14,15,] so let me just quickly recapitulate the main points of those earlier discussions:

- The libertarian state must consist of a central government, highly restricted in its powers so as to keep it from mischief, and a large number of competing local cantons, less restricted in their powers, so as to force political pressure down to the competitive canton level

[12]Roderick T. Long, "Virtual Cantons: A New Path to Freedom?," *Formulations*, Vol. I, No. 1 (Autumn 1993).

[13]Roderick T. Long, "Imagineering Freedom: A Constitution of Liberty" (Part I in *Formulations*, Vol. I, No. 4; Part II in Vol. II, No. 2; Part III in Vol. II, No. 3; Part IV in Vol. II, No. 4).

[14]Roderick T. Long, "The Rationale of a Virtual-Canton Constitution," *Proceedings of a Forum on the Subject of Constitutions* (2 October 1993).

[15]Roderick T. Long, "Assets and Liabilities of the Constitution of Oceania," *Proceedings of a Forum on the Subject of Constitutions* (2 October 1993).

lest it otherwise simply shatter the central government, or bypass it, or shape it to its will.

- The cantons should be "virtual" rather than physical; that is, membership in cantons should not be tied to geographical location; thus changing from one canton to another will be costless, thereby limiting the ability of cantons to oppress their members; anyone can change canton membership at will, and any sufficiently large number of citizens can start a new canton.

- Cantons should be almost entirely self-governing, appealing to the central government to solve inter-canton disputes only as a last resort.

- The central government should have a bicameral legislature — one house of canton representatives, empowered to pass laws but only by a supermajority, and a second house of popular representatives, empowered to repeal laws, with only a superminority being needed for such repeal.

- Laws should also be subject to repeal, and public officials subject to dismissal, by popular referendum.

- A plural executive should be instituted, to provide a check on presidential power. The plurality should be three rather than two, to resolve deadlocks in an emergency.

I've discussed other provisions, but these strike me as the most essential ones.

The Proprietary Model

A different libertarian structure is the proprietary community. In this case, the agency providing protective services is also the owner of the territory in which it will operate. This model too comes in two subvarieties, depending on whether a single person or firm owns all the territory and everyone else leases from the owner, or whether instead the territory is jointly owned by all the inhabitants. (The latter arrangement is called a commune when the inhabitants are hippies, and a condominium when the inhabitants are yuppies.)

This model has some disadvantages from a libertarian standpoint. One of the frustrations of statist society is that individuals have no place to stand on and call their *own*, no private property on which to do as they please without asking leave from others. Yet in a proprietary community, one's home is not really private; it belongs either to the landlord or to the collective. Since the arrangement is contractual, it satisfies libertarian standards of rights and justice — but perhaps not libertarian yearnings for independence.

Of course, it is possible to write the contract, and libertarians forming a proprietary community probably would so write it, in such a way as to make the leaseholds simulate private property as far as possible, to leave ample sphere for individuals to go their own way. But what guarantees that the contract will be respected? After all, the firm offering protective services, presumably including contract enforcement, is itself a party to the contract, and might decide to alter the terms unilaterally to its own advantage — thus turning into an oligarchic Leviathan. (Or, on the condominium model, the majority might decide to impose their will on the minority in defiance of the terms of the contract, thus turning into a democratic Leviathan.) Proponents of the proprietary model like to appeal to the example of hotels or apartment complexes; but hotel customers do not fear being oppressed by the manager, since they know there is a background of law enforcement to which the hotel manager must answer. But in a proprietary community, the hotel manager is also the chief of police.

Perhaps it will be said that the owners of a proprietary community will be restrained from abusing power by the fear of losing customers. But there is more than one way to prevent losing customers; one thinks of the Berlin Wall, for example.

The proprietary community model is also at a disadvantage, relative to the constitutionalist model, in dealing with other nations, which will treat a for-profit business enterprise with less respect than they would something that looks more like a sovereign state.

But the proprietary model has its advantages as well. Having a single firm control the territory can simplify the decision-making process, and income from leaseholds provides needed revenues to the "state" without the need for taxation. Perhaps most importantly, for those considering building a libertarian community at sea (or in space, for that matter), some kind of proprietary model may be unavoidable, at least for the territorial nucleus.

How can a proprietary community guard against the rise of Leviathan? There are several possibilities. One is to build into the contract something like the political structure of a virtual-canton constitution, as described above. Another is to separate the provision of security from the ownership of the territory; leaseholders might contract individually with a security company (or, preferably, with several competing security companies) rather than purchase their security through the landlord. Above all, it would be extremely foolish for residents in a proprietary community to contract away either the right to communicate freely (both with one another and with the outside world) or the right to own and carry weapons for self-defense. These two freedoms are the essential bulwark of liberty. To be sure, landlords have the right to place restrictions on the activities of their tenants; they can legitimately demand that everyone on their premises (other than themselves) be disarmed and refrain from unauthorized communication. But any tenant who agrees to live in the proprietary community on those terms is taking an unacceptable risk, in my view.

How is a proprietary community to gain respect in the eyes of other nations? One possibility is to build a community around a research station or a university; in conflicts with aggressor states, such a community would win more sympathy in world opinion than a community built around, say, a casino. Nor would it be the first time that an educational institution has acted as an autonomous political entity; the mediæval University of Bologna, for example, had its own student-run legal system, separate from that of the town of Bologna, and exercised civil and criminal jurisdiction over its own members.[16]

[16]Roderick T. Long, "A University Built by the Invisible Hand," in *Formulations*, Vol. I, No. 3 (Spring 1994).

The Pure Market Model

The third possible structure for a libertarian society is the pure market model. On this model, there is no central agency in charge — be it a minimal state, a dominant protection agency, or a landlord. Individuals own their own homes, and provision of legal services is not monopolized. I have defended this model in previous articles.[17,18,19,20]

The pure market model seems more vulnerable to Leviathans Past and Present than the constitutionalist and proprietary models, since it has nothing at all resembling a governmental face to turn to the outside world. Hence a libertarian society following such a model might have to be quite populous and powerful in order to succeed. This seems a serious disadvantage to market anarchism, at least in the short run.

On the other hand, the pure market model seems less vulnerable to Leviathan Yet to Come than does either the constitutionalist or the proprietary model, since those models all involve some monopolistic or near-monopolistic agency that is perfectly situated to turn itself into an oppressive state, whereas the pure market model involves no such agency. Nevertheless, many critics of the pure market model have argued that Leviathan would inevitably re-emerge.

---

[17]Roderick T. Long, "Implementing Private Law in a World of States," *op. cit.*

[18]Roderick T. Long, "The Nature of Law" (Part I in *Formulations*, Vol. I, No. 3; Part II in Vol. I, No. 4; Part III in Vol. II, No. 1).

[19]Roderick T. Long, "The Decline and Fall of Private Law in Iceland," in *Formulations*, Vol. I, No. 3 (Spring 1994).

[20]Roderick T. Long, "Anarchy in the U.K.: The English Experience with Private Protection," in *Formulations*, Vol. II, No. 1 (Autumn 1994).

Most versions of the pure market model envision a number of different agencies, specializing in protective services, and competing for clients. (As we shall see below, this is not the only form a pure market model might take.) Robert Nozick has argued, however, that any system of competing protection agencies would soon collapse into a monopolistic state.[21]

Nozick argues as follows: Competing protection agencies operating in the same territory will sometimes have conflicts. They will resolve these conflicts either by arbitration or by force. But in either case, the state will re-emerge.

Suppose two protection agencies resolve their disputes by resorting to force. Then either they are evenly matched, or one is stronger than the other. If one is stronger, then it will defeat the weaker one, either eliminating it or else making it subordinate to the victor. Where there were two agencies sharing one territory, there is now one agency for that territory; we have returned to territorial monopoly.

If instead the two agencies are evenly matched, and yet they continue to fight, clients of different agencies living in the same area will be motivated to relocate for security's sake. Two separate "turfs" will emerge, with one containing mostly clients of agency A, and the other mostly clients of agency B. Where there were two agencies sharing one territory, each agency now has its own territory; once again, we have returned to territorial monopoly.

In the first case, monopoly is achieved by uniting the agencies (or by eliminating one of them); in the second, it is achieved by dividing the territory. As many different protec-

---

[21] Robert Nozick, *Anarchy, State, and Utopia* (New York: Basic Books, 1974), Chapter 2.

tion agencies fight it out, each individual conflict between any two will resolve itself in one of the two ways outlined above, Nozick thinks; and the cumulative result of all the different conflicts will be some number of agencies, each holding a territorial monopoly. In other words, states.

Proponents of the market model generally regard it as unlikely that protection agencies would resolve their disagreement by force. In a competitive market, such agencies need to attract customers, and an agency that settles its disputes by expensive means, such as war, will have to charge higher premiums, and so will attract fewer customers, than a agency that settles its disputes by less expensive means, such as arbitration. Accordingly, such theorists argue, arbitration rather than violence will predominate.

Nozick denies none of this. But he argues that if protection agencies do opt for arbitration, the state will still re-emerge. For whatever system the agencies set up for resolving their disputes — courts of appeal, or what have you — will amount to the formation of a single legal system for the entire territory, and the individual protection agencies will then become no more than branches of this new structure. Where there were many agencies sharing one territory, there is now a single overarching agency for that territory; here too, then, we have returned to territorial monopoly.

To meet Nozick's argument, market anarchists must maintain that protection agencies could set up a dispute-resolution system that would be effective enough to prevent conflict, but would nevertheless fall short of constituting a new monopolistic agency. But a recent article by Tyler Cowen maintains that this is a vain hope.[22] Cowen argues that once competing

[22]Tyler Cowen, "Law as a Public Good: The Economics of Anarchy,"

protection agencies have set up a dispute-resolution network, the members of the network once it is established will be able to collude successfully to put competitors out of business. Ordinarily, such collusion would fail in a libertarian society, because new firms would have free entry into the market. But, points out Cowen, a new protection agency that is not part of the network cannot compete successfully with network members, since being a member of the network ensures that an agency will not have to go to war to secure its clients' claims. Customers will want the assurance of network membership before they sign up with a protection agency. But existing firms can simply choose to exclude from participation in their network any newcomer who doesn't toe the line. Hence, monopoly.

The most convincing reply I've seen to Cowan's argument is from Bryan Caplan.[23] Caplan makes two points against Cowan. First, Cowan neglects to consider the possibility of competing networks. In the credit card market, Visa providers have to cooperate with one another through the Visa network, and no new firm can succeed in acting as a Visa provider if it is excluded from the network; but the Visa network still has to compete with the Mastercard network and so forth. Likewise, one network of protection agencies might compete with two or three others. Cowan might reply that these networks too will need to cooperate with each other, and that this will lead to a new, meta-network; but Caplan disagrees. Protection agencies need to join a network

---

in *Economics and Philosophy*, Vol. 8 (1992), pp. 249-267. (See also the reply by David Friedman in the subsequent issue.)

[23]Bryan Caplan, "Outline of a Critique of Tyler Cowen's 'Law as a Public Good'," unpublished manuscript, July 1993.

to cut down on the transaction costs of contracting bilaterally with all the other agencies individually. But the number of networks is much smaller than the number of agencies, so transactions costs would not be high enough to warrant a new network; and with only bilateral contracts rather than a network, the capacity for collusion is quite small.

Caplan's second objection to Cowan's collusion scenario is that even if there were just one network, Cowan is too quick to assume that its attempts at collusion would be successful. Suppose two protection agencies, Titanic Defense and Hindenburg Security, come into conflict; Titanic is a member of the network, Hindenburg is not. But Hindenburg suggests submitting the dispute to arbitration. What is Titanic to do? The rules of the collusion agreement suggest that Titanic should refuse, that Titanic should resort to force instead. But this is expensive. And Hindenburg is even offering to pay the costs of arbitration. In such a case, Titanic has a strong incentive to defy the agreement and cooperate with Hindenburg. Of course, the other members of the network could boycott Titanic for doing this; but such a boycott is not in their interest either. Thus, Caplan suggests, attempts at collusion among protection agencies are likely to fail. Or, as I would put it, collusion among protection agencies is a form of selective cooperation, and so is likely to be undermined for the reasons I set out in my collective-action article.[24]

Finally, it's worth noting that both Nozick and Cowan think of the pure market model solely in terms of customers purchasing protective services on a competitive market. But

[24]Roderick T. Long, "Good and Bad Collective Action: Can We Nourish One and Squelch the Other?" *op. cit.*

this is not the only form that market anarchism can take. Another possibility is for customers to join together to provide for the common defense, rather than delegating this task to an agency. Such a arrangement is reminiscent of the mutual-protection associations common in English history.[25] The advantage of this self-help model is that it decreases the risk that protection agencies will get together to form a Leviathan. The downside, of course, is that self-help is time-consuming and can involve heavy transaction costs. But having such a self-help system in the background, ready to be mobilized if necessary, might help to keep the protection agencies in line, thus achieving the best of both worlds.

[25] Roderick T. Long, "Anarchy in the U.K.: The English Experience with Private Protection," in *Formulations*, Vol. II, No. 1 (Autumn 1994).

CHAPTER

TEN

MONOPOLY:
A NICE TRICK IF YOU CAN DO IT

KEVIN CARSON

One question that's frequently raised about market anarchism: How to prevent the economy from being taken over by monopolies, without anti-trust regulations and other restrictions on corporate abuses of power?

Without anti-trust laws, the argument goes, the firms in an oligopoly or cartel could simply lower prices when a competitor tried to enter the market, and then raise them again when the competitor went out of business.

Oligopoly firms could also, it's argued, use their market power to restrict competition in other ways, like making exclusivity contracts to prevent a would-be entrant to the same industry from obtaining the suppliers and outlets it needed to function.

---

http://c4ss.org/content/6256

The problem with this argument is that it assumes a great deal of what it needs to prove. Sure, prices are a lot stickier when you've got a stable oligopoly market. The Nader Group once estimated oligopoly markup at about 25% of total price in industries where half of output was controlled by four or fewer corporations. But how do you get an oligopoly market like that in the first place? Strategic underpicing is a lot more effective if the market is already divided up between a small number of big players — and this state of affairs seldom arises naturally.

The corporate revolution of the late 19th century presupposed several forms of massive state intervention: Railroad land grants, which made possible integration of the entire U.S. into a single market, and cartelization of industries through patent exchange and pooling. But even after the economy became dominated by giant corporations, argues Gabriel Kolko in *The Triumph of Conservatism*, attempts to establish cartels by purely private means were largely failures. The big trusts immediately began losing market share to smaller and lower-cost competitors.

It was this inability to maintain cartels by private means alone that sparked the Progressive Era's regulatory state, as corporations turned to government to suppress competition.

The tendency of cartels to break down into ruinous price wars was the reason for the "unfair competition" provisions of the Clayton and FTC Acts. Charging prices under cost was classed as unfair competition. According to Kolko, it was this provision that first made possible stable oligopoly markets in which firms competed in terms of brand-name image and fluff rather than price. That's right: The "Progressive" regulatory state was really working for the folks it regulated.

Ever hear the expression "Baptists and Bootleggers?" The biggest advocates for keeping a county dry, and the biggest source of campaign funds for temperance politicians, are the people who make money selling bootleg whiskey.

The effectiveness of strategic price-cutting to shut out competition also depends on entry costs — the size of the capital outlays required to build the first widget. The lower the entry costs, the more likely the dominant firm will find itself playing whack-a-mole, constantly having to resume the price war as competitors try to enter the market. That means that regularly selling below cost becomes a normal cost of business, raising the level of overhead for a dominant player trying to keep others out. In an environment where capital outlays to enter are low and the competitors keep coming and coming, that's a good way to go bankrupt.

Now consider, against this background, the fact that the capitalization costs required for market entry are not just a given. One major effect of government regulation is to raise capitalization levels, entry costs, and overhead in ways that protect incumbent producers and secure monopoly rents to them. It's a lot cheaper to shut out lower-cost competition if you've got a big buddy outlawing low-cost forms of production. Once again, the monopolists find a friend in the regulatory state.

As for exclusivity contracts, their effectiveness depends on the entry costs of becoming a supplier. Exclusivity contracts would present an opportunity for new entrants to collect a premium for being the first to serve the unmet needs. And they also offer a premium for defection by incumbent suppliers: If you're one of five suppliers for an industry, and the other four already have exclusivity contracts with the dominant incumbent player, which do you think offers the most promise: To become the fifth with an exclusivity contract, or to cut a deal with the new entrant?

All the envisioned monopoly strategies rely on the assumption that challengers would not adapt and develop workarounds ("the enemy usually has a plan, too — the dirty SOB!"). A primary effect of regulations is to criminalize those workarounds.

Monopoly is great, if you can just find a way to prevent competitors from entering the market and selling stuff cheaper than you. And when you penetrate behind the "progressive" aura of the regulatory state, you generally find it doing just that.

CHAPTER
ELEVEN

WHY MARKET EXCHANGE DOESN'T HAVE TO LEAD TO CAPITALISM

KEVIN CARSON

An anonymous reader of Center for a Stateless Society's *Tumblr*[1] recently asked:

> Two questions: 1) How exactly do the theory and practice proposed by free market anti-capitalists challenge the cultural logic of capitalism? 2) Don't all market institutions — whether a large corporation or a mom and pop shop — desire a state as part of the reproduction process?

The sheer scale of the cash nexus, compared to alternative models for organizing social life, and its growth at their expense, carries a lot of really bad imperatives with it. But

http://c4ss.org/content/29849

[1]http://c4ss.tumblr.com/

the scale of the cash nexus in corporate capitalism doesn't result from the existence of market exchange as such. There is every reason to believe that the elimination of entry barriers for self-employment and microproduction, and barriers to comfortable subsistence, would cause a radical shrinkage of the cash nexus. It would also result in transferring the way we meet a major portion of our needs either into small-scale exchange with other small producers in exchange networks that parallel social relations within our communities (like artisans in a pre-capitalist village[2]), or into non-monetized social production within extended family households and multi-family social units.

While economic calculation problems probably make market pricing necessary for coordinating large-scale production of widely-distributed goods or the extraction and distribution of raw materials like minerals, the proliferation of cheap micro-manufacturing tools[3] and the superior productivity of small-scale horticulture[4] would mean that such forms of large-scale production and long-distance distribution will rapidly shrink as a total part of the economy. One of the few absolutely necessary forms of large-scale production is the microprocessor industry. This and a few other things will require large-scale price coordination to allocate them over fairly large geographical regions.

The production of heavy internal combustion engine blocks, jet aircraft engines, molded car body panels that require three-story stamping presses, and the like, are also

[2]http://c4ss.org/content/21886

[3]http://opensourceecology.org/gvcs/

[4]http://www.sfgate.com/homeandgarden/article/THE-MAN-WHO-WOULD-FEED-THE-WORLD-John-Jeavons-2851481.php

things that require large-scale facilities serving large markets. But those things are mostly "necessary" in the first place only in response to artificially contrived needs[5] imposed on society by the existing power structure. As the Model T showed, a light internal combustion vehicle could function with an engine within the capability of a community machine shop today — not to mention small-scale manufacture of electric motors. Absent the Military-Industrial Complex's role in making civilian jumbo jets artificially profitable, large-scale air travel and freight would probably be done by lighter-than-air craft. And molded body parts, as opposed to a car design with flat panels produced on a cutting table, are a purely aesthetic product of Detroit.

In an economy without subsidized waste[6] or planned obsolescence,[7] and without the subsidies and props to the car[8] culture, probably 80% of total consumption needs could be produced either within a large household or multi-household social unit, or for money exchange at the neighborhood or small town level.

Rather than starting with extractive institutions and their logic, I'd start with the assumption of a society of people interacting with each other, who have needs to meet and skills to offer, and the arrangements they work out among themselves to bring those things together. Starting from this micro- level of individual cooperation and exchange, it's

[5]http://c4ss.org/content/24558
[6]http://c4ss.org/content/78
[7]http://c4ss.org/content/888
[8]http://c4ss.org/content/13083

easier to see how the removal of monopolies,[9] entry barriers[10] and artificial floors[11] under the cost of subsistence will have a liberating effect on those seeking to control their livelihoods and remove themselves from the wage system. Commenting on the reader's question, C4SS comrade Charles Johnson said:

> Everybody seems to think we're talking about "Mom and Pop" butcher stores or some other SBA client. I'm talking about the guy selling tacos at a roadside stand or fixing cars off the books in a vacant lot or hustling jobs on the day labor market or driving around a gypsy cab they own and operate or squatting a plot on a vacant lot to create the South Central Farm. A food coop or a commercial farm with a CSA is a big business in my world, not a small one. (And sure, sometimes big businesses are fine, I like my CSA.) The main target of my concern are the libraries of regulation that aim to choke off the ability to engage in commercial relationships at nano scale, in forms other than formalized mom/pop "small businesses."

This puts in a new light arguments of the kind frequent among market-skeptical or -hostile segments of the Left, either that the market carries structural imperatives to self-exploitation and the imposition of work-discipline even within cooperative and other forms of worker-controlled production, or that the existence of winners and losers within

[9] http://c4ss.org/content/4480
[10] http://c4ss.org/content/15533
[11] http://c4ss.org/content/3853

a non-capitalist market will result in the winners getting bigger and hiring the losers as wage laborers — thus essentially recreating capitalism and the wage system. A good statement of the problem comes from the P2P Foundation's email list by Marxist p2p theorist Christian Siefkes,[12] who sees commons-based peer production[13] as the core formation of a post-capitalist society:[14]

> Yes, they would trade, and initially their trading wouldn't be capitalistic, since labor is not available for hire. But assuming that trade/exchange is their primary way of organizing production, capitalism would ultimately result, since some of the producers would go bankrupt, they would lose their direct access to the means of production and be forced to sell their labor power. If none of the other producers is rich enough to hire them, they would be unlucky and starve (or be forced to turn to other ways of survival such as robbery/thievery, prostitution — which is what we also saw as a large-scale phenomenon with the emergence of capitalism, and which we still see in so-called developing countries where there is not enough capital to hire all or most of the available labor power). But, if there are other producers, people would hire them, the seed of capitalism with it's capitalist/worker divide is laid.

But in an economy of largely self-employed people or people cooperatively producing for direct self-provisioning

[12]http://p2pfoundation.net/Christian_Siefkes

[13]http://c4ss.org/content/22269

[14]http://peerproduction.net/issues/issue-1/invited-comments/beyond-digital-plenty/

within the social economy, there's no reason to have any permanent losers. The capital outlays are so low that it's possible to ride out a slow period indefinitely without any of the need for a constant revenue stream to service overhead like debt. And when the basic machinery for production is widely affordable and can be easily reallocated to new products, there's really no such thing as a "business" to go out of. The lower the capitalization required for entering the market, and the lower the overhead to be borne in periods of slow business, the more the labor market takes on a networked, project-oriented character — like, e.g., peer production of software. In free software, and in any other industry where the average producer owns a full set of tools and production centers mainly on self-managed projects, the situation is likely to be characterized not so much by the entrance and exit of discrete "firms" as by a constantly shifting balance of projects, merging and forking, and with free agents constantly shifting from one to another — or simply directly meeting their own needs through self-provisioning with an array of cheap general-purpose tools.

And in a society where most people own the roofs over their heads and can meet a major part of their subsistence needs through home production, workers who own the tools of their trade can afford to ride out periods of slow business, and to be somewhat choosy in waiting to contract out to the projects most suited to their preference. It's quite likely that, to the extent some form of wage employment still existed in a free economy, it would take up a much smaller share of the total economy, wage labor would be harder to find, and attracting it would require considerably higher wages; as a result, self-employment and cooperative ownership would be much more prevalent, and wage employment would be much more marginal. To the extent that wage employment continued, it would be the province of a class of itinerant laborers taking jobs of work when they needed a bit of supplementary income or to build up some savings, and then periodically retiring for long periods to a comfortable life living off their own homesteads. This pattern — living off the commons and accepting wage labor only when it was convenient — was precisely what the Enclosures were intended to stamp out.

In small cooperative firms operating within the local cash nexus, with low overhead and cheap tools, and a workforce with low household overhead and low income needs, workers are likely to choose work-sharing with reduced hours in preference to layoffs, and simply produce on whatever scale there's demand for at any time without any need to be forced "out of business." A local industrial district economy of networked small manufacturing cooperatives, or a project-based economy like the building trades or old-style longshoremen's hiring halls, presumes a solidaristic craft-based support network rather than the individual shop or job site as the primary economic unit. So the dislocations from economic downturns are far less severe.

Not to mention the downturns themselves are unlikely to be severe if they exist at all, where most money is circulated locally in local markets of small producers and production is closely tied to immediate demand. So arguments that markets carry some structural logic in favor of capitalism, or would inevitably lead to capitalism, implicitly assume a lot of characteristics of corporate capitalism as we know it as "normal."

CHAPTER

TWELVE

CAPITALISM, NOT TECHNOLOGICAL UNEMPLOYMENT, IS THE PROBLEM

KEVIN CARSON

At Slate, Will Oremus raises the question "What if technological innovation is a job-killer after all?" ("The New Luddites,"[1] August 6). Rather than being "the cure for economic doldrums," he writes, automation "may destroy more jobs than it creates":

> Tomorrow's software will diagnose your diseases, write your news stories, and even drive your car. When even high-skill "knowledge workers" are at risk of being replaced by machines, what human jobs will be left? Politics, perhaps — and, of course, entrepreneurship and management. The rich will

http://c4ss.org/content/30264

[1]http://www.slate.com/articles/technology/future_tense/2014/08/the_new_luddites_what_if_automation_is_a_job_killer_after_all.html

> get richer, in other words, and the rest of us will be left behind.

It's a common scenario, and one that's utterly wrong headed. Although Oremus appeals to Keynes' prediction of technological unemployment, the irony is that Keynes thought that was a good thing. Keynes predicted an economy of increasing abundance and leisure in his grandchildren's time, in which the average work week was fifteen hours.

Instead, as Nathan Schneider points out ("Who Stole the Four-Hour Workday?"[2] Vice, Aug. 5), US government policy since FDR's time has been to promote "full employment" at a standard 40-hr week. Both major parties, in their public rhetoric, are all about "jobs, jobs, jobs!"

This fixation on creating more work is what Bastiat, in the 19th century, called "Sisyphism" (after the lucky man in Hell who was fully employed rolling a giant rock up a hill for all eternity). We see the same ideological assumptions, as Mike Masnick argues in the same article where I got the Bastiat reference ("New Report Challenges The Whole 'IP Intensive Industries Are Doing Well Because Of Strong IP' Myth,"[3] Techdirt, Aug. 8), displayed in arguments that strong "intellectual property" law is necessary for creating "jobs" and guaranteeing income for creators.

The idea is that we either impose artificial inefficiencies on technologies of abundance in order to increase the amount of labor ("jobs!") required to produce a given standard of

[2]http://www.vice.com/read/who-stole-the-four-hour-workday-0000406-v21n8%20

[3]https://www.techdirt.com/articles/20140808/06392028146/new-report-challenges-whole-ip-intensive-industries-are-doing-well-because-strong-ip-claim.shtml

living, or we enclose those technologies to make their output artificially expensive so that everyone has to work longer hours to pay for them, so the increased price can go to paying wages for all those people running on conveyor belts and rat wheels. Make sense?

Either way, it amounts to hobbling the efficiency of new technology so that everyone has to work longer and harder than necessary in order to meet their needs. This approach is both Schumpeterian and Hamiltonian. Schumpeter saw the large corporation as "progressive" even when large size wasn't technically necessary for efficient production because, with its monopoly power, it could afford to fund expensive R&D and pass the cost on to consumers via cost-plus markup and administered pricing (basically like a regulated monopoly or Pentagon contractor). Mid-20th century liberalism, essentially a managerialist ideology that lionized large, hierarchical, bureaucratic organizations, extended this approach: the giant corporation could afford to pay high wages and maintain an employer-based welfare state, and still collect a guaranteed profit, because of its monopoly power.

Modern Hamiltonianism seeks to prevent price implosion from radical technological improvements in efficiency, and instead to guarantee inflated demands for both capital and labor — by imposing artificial inefficiency when necessary — so that returns on venture capital and full-time employment both remain stable.

The most egregious example is Jaron Lanier's argument that every bit of content anyone produces on the Web should be under strong copyright, so everyone can get paid for everything. But why stop there? Why not monetize the entire economy and force it into the cash nexus? Turn every single thing anybody does into a "job," so that members of a household get paid wages for mowing the lawn, washing the dishes, or vacuuming the living room. We could increase the nominal work week to 100 hours and per capita income to $100,000. That way, nobody would be able to obtain anything outside the cash nexus. They'd have to have a source of paid income to get the money to pay for anything they consumed — even a beer out of the fridge.

Ironically, that's the strategy European colonial powers used in Africa and the rest of the Third World to force native populations into the wage labor market and make it impossible to subsist comfortably without wage employment. They imposed a head tax that could only be paid in money, which meant that people who had been previously feeding, clothing and sheltering themselves in the customary economy were forced to go to work for wages (working for European colonial overseers who had appropriated their land, of course) in order to pay the tax.

It's utterly stupid. The whole point of the economy is not "jobs," but consumption. The point of human effort itself is consumption. The less effort required to produce a unit of consumption, the better. When a self-employed subsistence farmer figures out a way to produce the food she consumes with half as many hours of labor as before, she doesn't lament having "less work." That's because she internalizes all the benefits of her increased productivity. And when people are free to internalize both all the costs and all the benefits of increased productivity, so that improvements in efficiency are translated directly into lower prices or shorter working hours, they have an incentive to be more productive and work less.

The problem arises, not from the increased efficiency, but from the larger structure of power relations in which the increase in efficiency takes place. When artificial land titles, monopolies, cartels and "intellectual property" are used by corporations to enclose increased productivity as a source of rents, instead of letting them be socialized by free competition and diffusion of technique, we no longer internalize the fruits of technological advance in the form of lower prices and leisure. We get technological unemployment.

But technological unemployment and the rich getting richer are symptoms, not of the progress itself, but of the capitalistic framework of state-enforced artificial property rights and privilege within which it takes place. The economic ruling classes act through their state to intervene in the economy, to erect toll-gates and impede free market competition, so we have to work harder and longer than necessary in order to feed them in addition to ourselves. So let's not get rid of the technology. Let's get rid of the capitalists and their state that rob us of its full fruits.

CHAPTER
THIRTEEN

WHO OWNS THE BENEFIT?
THE FREE MARKET AS FULL COMMUNISM

KEVIN CARSON

There's a wonderful phrase for how capitalism works in the real world (I'm not sure who first came up with it, but I associate it with Noam Chomsky): "The socialization of risk and cost, and the privatization of profit."

That's a pretty good description of what the state does under actually existing capitalism, as opposed to the free market. Just about everything we identify as problematic about corporate capitalism — the exploitation of labor, pollution, waste and planned obsolescence, environmental devastation, the stripping of resources — results from the socialization of cost and risk and the privatization of profit.

Why haven't the cybernetic revolution and the vast increases in productivity from technological progress resulted

https://c4ss.org/content/12561

in fifteen-hour work weeks, or many necessities of life becoming too cheap to meter? The answer is that economic progress is enclosed as a source of rent and profit.

The natural effect of unfettered market competition is socialism. For a short time the innovator receives a large profit, as a reward for being first to the market. Then, as competitors adopt the innovation, competition drives these profits down to zero and the price gravitates toward the new, lower cost of production made possible by this innovation (that price including, of course, the cost of the producer's maintenance and the amortization of her capital outlays). So in a free market, the cost savings in labor required to produce any given commodity would quickly be socialized in the form of reduced labor cost to purchase it.

Only when the state enforces artificial scarcities, artificial property rights, and barriers to competition, is it possible for a capitalist to appropriate some part of the cost savings as a permanent rent. The capitalist, under these conditions, is enabled to engage in monopoly pricing. That is, rather than being forced by competition to price her goods at the actual cost of production (including her own livelihood), she can target the price to the consumer's ability to pay.

That form of enclosure, via "intellectual property," is why Nike can pay a sweatshop owner a few bucks for a pair of sneakers and then mark them up to $200. Most of what you pay for isn't the actual cost of labor and materials, but the trademark.

The same is true of artificial scarcity of land and capital. As David Ricardo and Henry George observed, there is some rental accruing on the natural scarcity of land as a non-reproducible good. There's considerable disagreement among Georgists, mutualist occupancy-and-use advocates, and other libertarians as to whether and how to remedy those natural scarcity rents. But artificial scarcity, based on the private enclosure and holding out of use of vacant and unimproved land, or on quasi-feudal landlord rights to extract rent from the rightful owners actually cultivating arable land, is an enormous source of illegitimate rent — arguably the major share of total land rent. And regardless of any other steps we may be advocate, principled libertarians are all in favor of abolishing this artificial scarcity and — at the very least — letting market competition from vacant land drive down land rent to its natural scarcity value.

We favor, as well, opening up the supply of credit to unfettered market competition, abolishing entry barriers for the creation of cooperative lending institutions, and abolishing legal tender laws of all kinds, so that market competition will eliminate a major portion of total interest on money.

But while demanding the socialization of rent and profit may be frowned upon by capitalists as "class warfare," they're totally OK with the socialization of their operating costs. The main reason modern production is so centralized and both firms and market areas are so large, is that the state has subsidized transportation infrastructure at the expense of the general public, and made it artificially cheap to ship goods long distance. This makes large-scale, inefficient producers artificially competitive against small-scale producers in the local markets they invade with the state's help. That's why we have giant retail chains driving local retailers out of business, using their own internalized "warehouses on wheels" wholesale operations to distribute goods manufactured by sweatshops in China.

The past forty years' loss of biodiversity, deforestation, and CO2 pollution has occurred because the ecosystem as a whole is an unowned dump, rather than being a regulated commons. The state typically preempts "ownership" of forests, mineral deposits, etc. — often to the prejudice of indigenous peoples already inhabiting the areas — and then gives privileged access to extractive industries that are able to strip mine them of resources without internalizing the actual costs incurred.

As surprising as it might seem, there's a strong parallel between this free market vision of abundance and the Marxist vision of full communism. Carl Menger wrote of economic goods (i.e., goods subject to economic calculation because of their scarcity) becoming non-economic goods (i.e., that their abundance and near-zero production cost would make the cost of accounting greater than the production cost, if any). This parallels a major strain of thinking among socialists in the free culture/open source/P2P movement. They see the communist mode of production practiced by Linux and other open-source developers as the kernel of a new post-capitalist, post-scarcity social formation. Much as capitalist production started out in tiny islands inside the larger feudal economy and later became the core of a new, dominant social formation, commons-based peer production is the core around which the post-capitalist economy will eventually crystallize.

And we free marketers are also information communists. We want the benefits of knowledge and technique to be fully socialized. The largest single share of profit under the current model of corporate capitalism is embedded rents on the artificial scarcity of knowledge and technique.

In a society where waste and planned obsolescence were no longer subsidized, and there were no barriers to competition socializing the full benefits of technological progress, we could probably enjoy our present quality of life with a fifteen-hour work week. And in a society where the dominant mode of production was craft production with cheap, general-purpose CNC machine tools (as Kropotkin anticipated over a century ago in Fields, Factories and Workshops), the division of labor and the dichotomy between mental and physical labor would be far less pronounced.

Taken together, these two outcomes of free market competition in socializing progress would result in a society resembling not the anarcho-capitalist vision of a world owned by the Koch brothers and Halliburton, so much as Marx's vision of a communist society of abundance in which one may "do one thing today and another tomorrow, to hunt in the morning, fish in the afternoon, rear cattle in the evening, criticise after dinner, just as I have a mind, without ever becoming hunter, fisherman, herdsman or critic."

PART II

∞

"Free Markets & Capitalism?"

C4SS's October 2015 Mutual Exchange

CHAPTER

ONE

WILL FREE MARKETS RECREATE CORPORATE CAPITALISM?

KEVIN CARSON

Some anarchists and socialists argue that, even if markets can theoretically be non-capitalist, and non-capitalist market economies can exist, the dynamics of the market will eventually lead to the restoration of capitalism. The argument used by non-market anarchists and socialists is that, in a competitive market — even a competitive market of widespread distribution of the means of production and mostly self-employment or cooperative production — there will be winners and losers. The losers will go out of business, and go to work as wage laborers for the winners who buy them out. A typical statement of this argument is that of Christian Siefkes, a libertarian Marxist associated with the P2P Foundation (quoted from their email discussion list):

https://c4ss.org/content/40154

> Yes, they would trade, and initially their trading wouldn't be capitalistic ... But assuming that trade/exchange is their primary way of organizing production, capitalism would ultimately result, since some of the producers would go bankrupt, they would lose their direct access to the means of production and be forced to sell their labor power. If none of the other producers is rich enough to hire them, they would be unlucky and starve ... which is what we also saw as a large-scale phenomenon with the emergence of capitalism, and which we still see in so-called developing countries where there is not enough capital to hire all or most of the available labor power). But if there are other producers/people [who would] hire them, the seed of capitalism with its capitalist/worker divide is laid.

The question, then, is whether a competitive marketplace without capitalistic distortions would, entirely through peaceful exchange, eventually be transformed into one with large concentrations of wealth and the predominance of wage labor. I argue that it would not.

Before I continue I should clarify some points: Coming from the individualist anarchist tradition of Thomas Hodgskin and Benjamin Tucker, I distinguish "capitalism" here from the free market, as a system in which the political and economic system is controlled by capitalists, and the state intervenes in the market on their behalf; a capitalist market, as opposed to a free one, is characterized by artificial property rights, artificial scarcities, subsidies and monopolistic entry barriers or cartels.

And when I say "free markets," I am not referring to a society in which the majority of economic functions are organized through money exchange (the "cash nexus") or business firms. By "free market" I mean only a society in which money exchange is allowed as part of the mix, not any particular specification as to how big a component of the mix it might be. In fact I think it's quite likely that a far greater share of economic needs than at present would be met, in a free society, through non-market activities like direct production for use within the informal and household sector, direct subsistence production in larger co-housing units and neighborhood multi-family collectives, or networked "commons-based peer production"; and a major share of natural resources would be owned under the kinds of commons governance regimes Elinor Ostrom devoted so much analysis to. As both employer-based and government-based safety nets erode and corporations and governments retreat from the social sphere, I expect a growing share of economic life to be governed through voluntary, communal organizations for pooling risk, costs and income on models similar to the guilds and fraternal societies and the open field villages of the later Middle Ages (which figured so prominently in Kropotkin's historical work). In this regard I refuse to include Siefkes's stipulation of exchange as the main way of organizing production, as part of the definition of "market economy."

All that being said, I'll return to the original question: Would the existence of free markets inevitably lead to the revival of capitalism, wealth concentration and the wage system, or to a corporate economy dominated by a small number of giant business organizations? To repeat, I say it wouldn't.

To take the question of the corporate economy first, the typical argument — in my experience coming from liberals and Center-Left types in venues like *Salon* or the comments at *Daily Kos* — is that the Gilded Age was a time of "laissez-faire" that spontaneously gave rise to the era of giant trusts. The Progressive reforms at the turn of the 20th century were passed to bring the unbridled corporate economy that grew out of it back under control.

But the corporate economy as we know it did not emerge naturally as the result of market forces; it was a creature of the state. The large-scale system of long-distance railroad trunk lines in the U.S., which rendered long-distance shipping artificially cheap and created artificially large market areas and artificially large firms to serve them, came about through the railroad land grants. This high-capacity national railroad system was a prerequisite for the ecosystem of national wholesale and retail operations that grew up around it, which in turn were prerequisites for the rise of national manufacturing corporations that grew up to serve the newly created continental market. Even Alfred Chandler, an enthusiastic defender of the centralized mass-production industrial model of the 20th century, conceded that centralized nationwide distribution and then production were possible only because of the state's role in creating a high-capacity nationwide transportation system.

Absent such intervention, the railroad system would likely have taken the form — as Lewis Mumford argued — of a large number of local networks loosely patched together with a much lower capacity system of national trunk lines. And the ideal form of industrial production for such a loose federation of local railroad networks would have been the industrial district model.

In addition, the industrial tariff served as a wall behind which it was easier to cartelize industry. And the exchange and pooling of patents was also a powerful cartelizing tool (for example, the origins of A&T as the Bell family patent system, the cartelization of the consumer appliance industry by GE and Westinghouse's exchange of patents, the formation of RCA by pooling the patents of the five leading U.S. radio producers, etc.). Finally, the most important effect of the Progressive Era regulatory state was to permit stable oligopoly industries for the first time by restricting price and quality competition; the Federal Trade Commission, which for its first two decades treated selling below cost and other price-war tactics as "unfair competition" was especially significant in this regard.

The ideal technical application of the electrically powered machinery enabled by the invention of the electric generator and electric motor would have been the above-mentioned industrial district system: Craft production using relatively cheap, electrically powered, general-purpose machinery to produce for local markets, frequently changing from one product line to another as orders came in, on a lean/just-in-time/demand-pull basis. The cumulative effect of all the state interventions listed above was to divert this technological current into an entirely different channel: Mass-production using expensive, large-scale, product-specific machinery and producing enormous runs of the same product for national distribution on a supply-push, batch-and-queue basis.

In short, the large-scale corporate economy that arose in the 19th century was very much — to repeat — a creature of the state.

Moving further back, to the origin of the capitalist system itself, I argue that it was likewise entirely a creature of the state. The concentration of wealth and predominance of wage labor did not arise from a free market; massive state coercion was involved in its creation.

First of all, in the only history we know, systems in which the means of production are mostly owned by a small wealthy class and the majority of the population works for wages did not come about through the peaceful process of sorting winners from losers in a competitive market. They came about through large-scale force. And in particular, the engrossment of enormous tracts of land in a few hands has come about only through robbery. The capitalist system of early modern Western Europe was a direct outgrowth of the "bastard feudalism" of late medieval times. A major part of the landed aristocracy reinvented themselves as agrarian capitalists. The new absolute states, reflecting a constellation of interests that included the landed classes, the mining and armaments industries, and the chartered monopolies, nullified the peasant majority's customary rights in the land, and either transformed them into agricultural wage laborers or rack-rented and evicted them. With their new gunpowder armies they militarily defeated the free, self-governing town communes. The process culminated in Britain, on the eve of the Industrial Revolution, with the Parliamentary Enclosure of common wood, fen and pasture, and the same drama was reenacted on a global scale starting with Hastings's Permanent Settlement in Bengal. By the end of the 19th century the mineral wealth of Africa and Oceania had been looted by Western mining companies, and much of the best arable land appropriated by European settlers.

The great capitalist fortunes that funded the Industrial Revolution in Britain belonged to the Whig landed oligarchs who inherited the fruits of robbery and Enclosure, and to the mercantile profiteers associated with chartered monopolies of various sorts. The industrial working class that worked the new factories was supplied by the former peasants, who had already been forcibly transformed into a propertyless proletariat through the Enclosures.

And the institutional forms of the Industrial Revolution — the factory system and the wage system — took shape in an environment of police state repression. The Laws of Settlement in Britain amounted to an internal passport system prohibiting the working class from travelling from parish to another without the permission of the Poor Law authorities. So inhabitants of overpopulated parishes were unable to "vote with their feet" by moving elsewhere in search of better employment opportunities. Although at first glance this would seem to work counter to the needs of factory owners in the sparsely populated areas of the industrial north and west, the authorities — having prevented the population from travelling on their own and negotiating to fill vacancies — filled the vacancies themselves by auctioning off the destitute surplus population to employers. Besides this, the Combination Laws and a whole body of police state legislation against friendly societies prevented workers from freely associating to increase their bargaining power. So the state mandated that workers take whatever employers offered or leave it, with no freedom to bargain for higher wages — and then acted as bargaining agent on behalf of employers.

Second, the coercion isn't just a matter of past history, whether the early days of capitalism or of the industrial revolution. In our actual history, the fortunes resulting from those original acts of robbery have continued to grow upon themselves throughout the capitalist era through the "magic of compound interest" — the result of monopoly rates of rent, interest and profit possible only because of artificial scarcities and artificial property rights enforced by the state.

Natural property rights are rights to one's own possessions and labor products; they reflect natural scarcity, and enforcement in the first instance follows directly from the act of physical possession itself (physically occupying and using a piece of land, retaining physical custody of things one has produced, etc.). Artificial property rights, on the other hand, enable the holder to a portion of the labor product of others, by creating artificial scarcity where it would not naturally exist. A legally privileged class of people is able, in the words of Henry George Jr., to obstruct access to natural opportunities or erect toll-gates to the use of things that should be naturally free and abundant. The classic example is the landlord who encloses vacant and unoccupied land and charges tribute for the right to cultivate or build on it.

Absent artificial scarcities of land and credit, and barriers to market entry for firms, most remaining profit would be short-term and entrepreneurial from the "first mover advantage" of introducing an innovation or being the first to move a resource where it is needed, and would quickly be destroyed by competition as others adopt the innovation or follow the same price signals. Profit would be self-liquidating.

Another major example is so-called "intellectual property," which amounts on a restriction on using one's own labor to transform material resources in one's own possession because someone "owns" the pattern into which one wants to organize those resources. And a whole host of laws restricts the supply of money and credit to a privileged class, and thereby makes them artificially scarce and expensive.

But the general category includes all entry barriers and restraints on free competition: Zoning laws that protect established businesses from competition from home-based micro-enterprise; regulations that impose capital outlay requirements on undertaking production over and above those actually required by technical necessity; licensing regimes that restrict the numbers of competing providers in a market or limit market entry to those able to pay a large licensing fee; regulations whose main purpose is to artificially increase the cost of entering the market, so that only big players can participate; "safety" codes written by the regulated industries whose primary purpose is to prevent the adoption of new, cheaper production technologies (a good example is housing codes written by building contractors that exclude vernacular building techniques and new, low-cost technologies for self-built housing, and thereby put a floor under the minimum cost of comfortable subsistence).

More broadly, the category extends to all forms of guard labor, planned obsolescence and subsidized waste, and all restraints on competition that make the market safe for large, inefficient bureaucracies with high overhead that, in Ivan Illich's words, increase the cost of making and doing anything by 300% or 400%. And this 300% or 400% increase goes entirely to a class of parasitic rentiers. And it includes the "radical monopolies," to use another good term of Illich's, that render people artificially dependent on the output of some industry (the classic example is subsidies to freeways and regulatory mandates to sprawl and monoculture development, which make it impossible to access work and shopping by foot, bicycle or streetcar and transform the automobile into a necessity of life).

In every case, the principle is what Thorstein Veblen called "serviceable disserviceability": Collecting tribute for the "service" of not obstructing production. It should go without saying that none of these things — all of which were involved in transferring wealth upwards from the producing population and concentrating it in the hands of a small propertied class — would be permitted in a society based on voluntary association and free exchange.

But besides all that, new production technologies are rendering earlier distinctions between being "in business" and "out of business," or between being "employed" and "unemployed," increasingly meaningless — and in the process rendering obsolete the whole idea of a capitalist wage system emerging from the process of winners and losers.

Not that sorting itself is bad — competition that causes people to shift from things they're comparatively worse at to things they're better at is good, so long as 1) there are no harsh, abrupt dislocations; 2) people are cushioned and able to ride out periods of change comfortably; and 3) there is no permanent class of losers.

And there is indeed no reason to have any permanent losers. First of all, the overhead costs are so low that it's possible to ride out a slow period indefinitely. Second, in low-overhead flexible production, in which the basic machinery for production is widely affordable and can be easily reallocated to new products, there's really no such thing as a “business” to go out of. The lower the capital requirement for entering the market, and the lower the overhead to be borne in periods of slow business, the more the labor market takes on a networked, project-oriented character — like, e.g., peer production of software. In free software, and in any other industry where the average producer owns a full set of tools and production centers mainly on self-managed projects, the situation is likely to be characterized not so much by the entrance and exit of discrete “firms” as by a constantly shifting balance of projects, merging and forking, and with free agents constantly shifting from one to another. In addition, in a society where most people own the roofs over their heads and can meet a major part of their subsistence needs through home production and sharing or exchange with their neighbors, workers who own the tools of their trade can afford to ride out periods of slow business, and to be somewhat choosy in waiting to contract out to the projects most suited to their preference.

CHAPTER

TWO

CORPORATE CAPITALISM: NOT SIMPLY A PRODUCT OF THE STATE

DEREK WALL

My background is in ecosocialism. I am not an anarchist; in fact, I am currently International Coordinator of the Green Party of England and Wales. I would see ecosocialism as rooted in Marxist thought. So unsurprisingly I would tend to argue that non-capitalist markets tend to lead to the restoration of capitalism.

However, my polemic with Kevin is going to be blunted for three reasons. First, while I was mystified by the existence of free market left anarchism, I have had some education on the matter. While I am neither an anarchist nor an advocate of markets, I would agree, surprisingly perhaps, with much of Kevin's analysis. We are both keen followers of Elinor Ostrom, whose perspectives are absolutely essential to me.

---

https://c4ss.org/content/40724

Second, I do not adhere to a model of social change based on pure knowledge. Winning an intellectual argument is not the same as creating social change; debates like this are useful but are no substitute for applied practical action. There is a kind of gnostic Leninism that argues that correct intellectual positions are almost everything. I don't agree. Third, I live with my wife in a trailer, we brew beer, and currently have about one hundred bottles of IPA, Pilsner and wheat beer. To some extent I was inspired to begin brewing by Kevin's homebrew revolution. I have a materialistic perspective, and what can be more material than large quantities of home produced beer? This gives me a warm feeling whenever I see the words 'Kevin Carson'. Nonetheless I have enough disagreement to make a debate, but I am not going to be calling anybody foolish and I will attempt to resist being dogmatic in my assertions here.

We certainly have a common enemy. Corporations dominate both economics and politics, concentrating power in their hands and encroaching on more and more of daily life. A fictional but clear illustration can be found David Foster Wallace's novel *Infinite Jest.* Years are no longer numerical but are named by corporations as a form of sponsorship and advertising as part of the "Chronology of organization of North American nations" revenue-enhancing subsidized time. The "Years" include Year of the Whopper, Year of the Tucks Medicated Pad, Year of the Trial-Size Dove Bar and so on to the year of the Depend Adult Undergarment and the Year of Glad. Corporations seem to impose an ever growing invasion of daily life and can be contrasted, apparently, with more innocent and constrained competitive markets. It is easy to see markets as normal and corporate markets as absurd and unnatural.

The writer David Korten argued that the relationship between a competitive market and corporate capitalism is like the relationship between a healthy body and a cancer. Markets are natural and beneficial in his view, but monopolies are not. They are the poisonous outgrowth of a healthy system. While I think Kevin's approach is much, much more nuanced than Korten's, I think this is a good starting point for debate. I would argue that the relationship between markets and corporate capitalism is more like a chicken and an egg. Markets tend, in largely spontaneous ways, to generate capitalism.

I think there are number of arguments to suggest that if we replaced corporate control with market competition, we would, in a relatively short time, be back to concentrated markets. I am, incidentally, a market skeptic; I tend to feel that any market is to a large extent oppressive and ecologically destructive, but that is part of a larger and perhaps more difficult debate than can be completed here.

Marx argued, I feel correctly, that there is a tendency for capital to become concentrated. Whatever the intention of market agents, competition tends to lead to the removal of smaller enterprises and a drive to monopoly. Even ignoring Marx, it is clear that traditionally, and I know that Kevin challenges this in an interesting way, economies of scale mean larger firms often drive out smaller. Internal economies of scale occur when increased output leads to falling average costs in the long term. Bulk buying reduces average costs for raw materials. Market power pushes down wages and prevents better uses of machinery and storage, which leads to falling overall average costs which can be used to drive out higher cost, smaller producers.

Marx argued in *Capital* that human labour power tends to be replaced by non-human capital. This has a number of implications. One is that the firms that invest first in new technologies tend to drive out those firms that don't. Technological innovation with increased investment tends to lead to market concentration. This contrasts sharply with the libertarian view (to the extent as a non-libertarian that I understand it) that market power is a product largely of legal barriers created by the state.

Brewer, in his handy guidebook *Marxist Theories of Imperialism*, summarizes Marx's view:

> Constant efforts to cut costs are forced on capitalists by competition, the primary driving force in capitalism. Any new method of production which reduces costs (a technical improvement, or an 'improvement' in labour discipline) will bring extra profits to those who introduce it quickly, before the general price level has been forced down. Once it is generally adopted, competition forces prices down in line with costs, wiping out any remaining high cost producers. Marx assumed (in general rightly) that large scale-production is more efficient than small-scale. Competition therefore forces capitalists to accumulate and reinvest as much as possible in order to produce on a large scale. Marx called growth through reinvestment of profits, *concentration of capital.* Bigger firms will be better able to survive, especially in slumps, and will be able to buy out smaller firms. The growth of the scale of production by amalgamation of capitals is called *centralization*

of capital.[1]

Markets also tend to encroach on more and more of human life. We haven't got to the point where years are sponsored by corporations, but no doubt the moon will be used as an advertising billboard and our lives are increasingly spent in corporate space. Kurt Vonnegut's novel *Cat's Cradle* illustrates this with the concept of Ice Nine. In the book, Ice Nine is invented to help the US marines do battle. It is a fictional kind of ice with a chemical twist: When it comes into contact with water, it turns the water into ice. The idea is that the marines can drop ice nine into a river and create an instant bridge to move forward. The unintended consequence is that ice nine can never stop turning water into ice. If ice nine were to be used it would eventually turn all of the world's water into ice, extinguishing life. In the novel, a chip of Ice Nine is held in a thermos flask, but inevitably it is released and life on earth is destroyed. Money tends to move into new areas of society with exchange value taking over more and more of human life. Money may not be Ice Nine, but it does tend to corrode non-market systems into money. Cash infiltrates more and more of society, so competitive markets, rather being natural and nonviolent, have increasingly totalitarian consequences.

Corporations seem to have cultural capital too. We can see Facebook, Uber, Twitter and other forms of web-based commons using cash to expand, floating on markets and squeezing out alternatives. Amazon is another example. In short, it is not enough to see corporations as purely a product of government intervention; there are additional powerful

[1]1990: 33.

forces that tend to lead to market concentration.

Finally, I think Hegel noted somewhere that it is impossible to leap over one's age. In a society even where we try to imagine alternatives, our dreams are powerfully conditioned by the world we exist within. We never have pure free will with which to design other ways of being. What we can imagine is limited by social forces that are often to a large extent unconscious, and even where we can mentally make a leap, material conditions limit what we can achieve. I think the literary theorist Raymond Williams argued that in this sense, utopias are more compensatory than emancipatory. We map alternatives as a substitute because our attempts to practically challenge the rich and powerful are impotent.

Elinor Ostrom once described how, as a school student, she was encouraged to join the debating society. She recounted how members of the society would argue one side of the debate and then change sides to debate the other. I believe this gave her considerable mental flexibility, and to some extent, with her pragmatic grassroots approach, she was able to envision some very radical things about political economy. I am not (Ostrom fan that I am) going to use this method and argue against my own points and suggest markets may not lead to corporate capitalism. Nonetheless, to move things forward I am going to look at some alternative perspectives. What is the point of Marxism if you cannot embrace contradiction?

Marx generally examined countervailing tendencies to the process that he sought to describe. Far from outlining a theological or deterministic system, he was aware that multiple factors, including intentional human agency, might blunt or reverse likely change. Equally in his late Russian discussion, where he toyed with the idea of the Russian communal farming system (the Mir) as providing a way of reaching communism without a capitalist stage, he suggested that his work in *Capital* might only be applicable to Western Europe. So while both theoretical argument and empirical evidence suggest that his argument for capital concentration is sound, counter tendencies are possible. Certainly Kevin has made a strong case for the fact that diseconomies of scale may mean that small scale production is cost efficient. Equally, in an era of fast evolving 3D printing and web-based advances, open source manufacturing may reverse any apparent historical trend.

Neither should we be technological determinists; to my view Marxism is an intellectual network approach with institutional, economic, ecological and social class all interacting. All history may be the history of class struggle but a range of factors including the legal come into play. I reject the idea that capital concentration is always and everywhere an effect of government action. However, institutional factors do shape economics. Companies seek to create barriers to competition and governments often help them. Concentration cannot, I feel, be explained purely as a product of governments manipulating otherwise competitive markets, but governments do contribute to corporate rule. In fact, any economy has an institutional element.

Kevin and I are perhaps starting off from different perspectives, close too, in the kind of non-corporate economy we both want to see. While he sees value in markets, he does to some extent over-leap the conventional assumptions, like both Marx and Ostrom, recognising that economic activity extends beyond markets and states. This position is vitally important because there is a large and increasingly militant rebellion against corporate neoliberalism taking place. In Europe, parties like Podemos and Syriza have risen on opposition to austerity and corporate control. I am still amazed that my friend Jeremy Corbyn, a lonely left wing MP who was more popular with Greens than his own party, has won a landslide victory to lead the opposition Labour Party here in the UK. In Rojava and the rest of Kurdistan, the revolutionary Kurds, learning from their own participatory experiments and the writings of green anarchist Murray Bookchin, are creating a left libertarian non-state.

The forces for change are rising. The debate around markets and corporations can have a modest but material effect on the change that occurs. Rather than simply dismissing Kevin Carson's view, I would note that the kind of diverse market-plus-commons economy he, and indeed Elinor Ostrom, advocated, risks turning back into capitalism. To avoid this will require precise mechanism, perhaps some kind of jubilee as advocated in the Torah for wiping out debt and redistributing resources. Nonetheless, this vision of democratic ownership of the means of production is close to that of Marx. Marxists, in rejecting the market have, instead of creating a stateless society, often tended to recreate statist societies. While we cannot at a stroke move beyond both markets and states, we can I believe to some extent, roll both markets and states back, democratize the economy and create institutional governance which is participatory rather than elitist.

Finally, a heretical thought is that Kevin's observation that corporate control involves violence through primitive accumulation is, of course, Marx's view too. In Chapters 26 and 27, Marx hints, in contradiction to much of the rest of his work, that markets based on personal, broadly democratic ownership are possible. With the breakdown of feudalism, a measure of freedom existed but was snuffed out in England by the violence of enclosure. Rothbard, Marx and Carson have some shared perspectives; no wonder Kevin's work is threatening and too often ignored both by left and right.

In summary, I don't think corporate capitalism is simply a product of state-created legal barriers. This is part of the story but there are other forces that tend to promote monopoly. Equally, I don't see markets as a panacea. However, like Kevin, I want to promote a diverse economy that moves beyond the state and the market to the commons. Last, much of Kevin's analysis mirrors readings of Marx that suggest that democratic ownership of the means of production is essential to a more equal and ecological future.

CHAPTER

THREE

WILL TRULY FREE MARKETS BE TRULY DIFFERENT?

STEVEN HORWITZ

There is much to like in Kevin Carson's lead essay and even where I think he goes astray, he performs a valuable service by reminding us of the ways in which the state has affected the evolution of really-existing capitalism and he thereby challenges us to think more critically and expansively about what a truly free market might look like.

One of the most important points Carson makes is something of a throwaway at the start, namely the claim that the "free market" need not mean only, or even primarily, that social cooperation takes places through the "cash nexus." Instead, it simply allows such relationships as one among a whole range of ways in which humans can voluntarily cooperate to solve their problems, whether through markets

https://c4ss.org/content/40822

or friendly societies or houses of worship or any of an array of other organizational forms that might arise in a free society. This is a point often overlooked by both libertarians and their critics. A free society is much more than a giant marketplace. One of the strengths of Carson's essay, and his work more generally, is to remind us that the omnipresence of the state for so much of human history has often limited our imagination about what a free society might look like, both in its narrowly economic relationships and all the other ways humans interact.

This, I will note, is one reason why the work of the Ostroms, who Carson briefly mentions, is so important. Both Lin and Vincent Ostrom challenge the market/state dichotomy from different angles and thereby also force us to think more creatively about what a free society really means. Lin's work asks us to consider the variety of forms that managing the commons can take, with special attention paid to how communities might create rules and norms for doing so. What's interesting about that work is that it is about *governance* more than *government.* To the degree the community collectively and voluntarily agrees to a set of rules, it looks like something other than the market or state as we typically know them. It is a political solution to an economic problem, but it is not the sort of top-down regulation we get from states. As Carson notes, we might well get much more of these sorts of community-based institutional solutions in a free society, particularly on a local scale.

Vincent's work asks us to consider that "democracy" is more than elections and legislatures, but instead refers to the participatory way that each of us negotiates with each other to develop rules of social conduct. Each time people avoid or resolve conflicts by working with others to solve the problem at hand, they are engaged in the task of democracy. Like Lin's work, this is about developing rules for solving problems. For Vincent, the more interesting problems were often smaller scale ones, such as the more routine conflicts that characterize our day-to-day existence.

The Ostroms shared the concern that community-based solutions to commons problems and our ability to avoid and resolve small-scale conflicts were being crowded out by both the state and the market (in Carson's sense of the "cash nexus"). These other forms of human cooperation were being crushed from both sides by the regulatory state and narrow conceptions of economic institutions. One way of reading this opening point from Carson is that a truly free society opens up that middle ground to a range of Ostrom-style organizational forms. A free market need not be only markets. And an anarchist society is not without governance. The institutional forms that emerge may look much more like the ones we associate with civil society, and Carson rightly notes they are likely to play a much bigger role in a free society.

The problems with Carson's argument are the same ones that seem to infect much left-libertarian writing: too many assertions without careful economic argument about what a truly free market would look like and simultaneously overstating, in my view, the distortions created by the state by ignoring the underlying economics. Before I give a couple of particulars, let me note that I don't deny the general claims. The state has certainly distorted the way in which markets have evolved and thereby affecting the kinds of institutions and economic arrangements that define the status quo. And

I do think a truly free market would look different from the status quo. What I am much more skeptical about is the *degree* of those differences.

There is no doubt that the interventions of governments at various levels have subsidized aspects of the current structure of the US economy, as Carson points out. The state's role in building interstate highways and the railways certainly enabled producers to externalize the costs of transportation onto others. Carson concludes from this that such large-scale transportation systems would not exist in a free society (or would not have existed had we been a free society) and that economies would be more regional and local. Perhaps. It is always worth reminding left-libertarians that you can't prove a counter-factual. In addition, it is not clear why he so quickly dismisses the possibility that ensuring the existence of such transportation systems to facilitate a nationwide market might not be worth it for the private sector.

Think about the ways in which Walmart benefits from infrastructure subsidies. They are certainly happy to do so, of course, but if those subsidies didn't exist, it might well be worth it for Walmart to bear the costs themselves, or to develop cooperative arrangements with other producers, if the projected revenues were sufficient. Perhaps that might mean higher production costs for Walmart, but it would also mean much lower property taxes. It is not as obvious as Carson seems to think it is that the private sector would not replicate something close to what we have now. Interestingly, one way they might do so is through inter-firm institutional or organizational arrangements that display the sort of commons management that Lin Ostrom's work discusses.

Carson also makes a similar kind of assertion about electrical machinery: "The ideal technical application of the electrically powered machinery enabled by the invention of the electric generator and electric motor would have been the above-mentioned industrial district system: Craft production using relatively cheap, electrically powered, general-purpose machinery to produce for local markets, frequently changing from one product line to another as orders came in, on a lean/just-in-time/demand-pull basis." I can see no meaningful argument or evidence to support this assertion. It might be true, but there's no reason to think so that I can see. It strikes me as a bit of wishful thinking whereby Carson is able to draw a much greater contrast between the capitalist status quo and his idealized free society.

One last point of economics for Carson to consider. At the end, he argues that in a truly free market we would see less of the sort of unemployment and "going out of business" that we see today thanks to the fluidity of a market with lower capital requirements for entry in smaller-scale production. What Carson appears to misunderstand here is the nature of capital goods, at least in the eyes of the Austrian economists. Even where the scale of production is smaller, "capital" in the abstract does not exist, in contrast to the implication Carson leaves by referring to "capital requirements." Capital comes in the form of specific goods with a limited number of productive uses, not all of which deliver the same value. The same is true of human capital. The fact that it takes less investment to start a business in a smaller-scale economy doesn't help much when even the smaller-scale machinery that a firm uses cannot be costlessly refit to new uses when demands change or competition favors other firms. The same is true of people. They cannot costlessly "refit" their human capital in the face of exogenous change. Even if production is at smaller scale, inevitable economic change will require costly and time-consuming adjustments by capital and labor, leaving some capital idle and some labor unemployed for some period of time. Perhaps those time periods will be smaller, but again absent more argument, that would be mere assertion. But thinking the length of idleness would approach zero is precisely the sort of utopianism of which left-libertarianism is too often guilty.

As I have argued before, I find it a very convenient coincidence that the left-libertarian picture of a free market society just happens to line up almost exactly with the world that many on the traditional left desire. Eliminating all the influence that the state might have does not magically transform all of the stuff the left doesn't like about really-existing capitalism into alternative arrangements that they (would) like. It is an open question how much statism it takes to conclude that the truly free market will look very little like actual capitalism. It's my own belief that the underlying economic processes matter more for the relevant costs and benefits than do the distorting effects of the state, and along more margins, than the left-libertarians believe. I might well be wrong, but the danger for the left-libertarians is that they are making the same sort of utopian (in the bad sense) promises that have been made by the traditional left. If people are skeptical of that utopianism, it may also backfire onto more mainstream libertarians.

Kevin Carson's essay reminds us not to succumb to what some have called "vulgar libertarianism" in taking the status quo as evidence for what a free society would look like. At the same time, though, that reminder can turn into an equally unproductive utopianism that makes promises that have little evidence to support them and are therefore unlikely to be kept.

CHAPTER

FOUR

CAPITALISM DEPENDS ON ARTIFICIAL, STATE-ENFORCED STABILITY

KEVIN CARSON

I appreciate the thoughtful tone of Derek's response, and I'm certainly gratified by whatever role I may have played in inspiring him to take up brewing beer. And having been strongly influenced by the work of Elinor Ostrom myself, I was pleased to learn that an Ostrom scholar was invited to respond to my article for this symposium.

As for his actual argument, I think his restatement of my positions is quite fair. Despite the friendly tone of his counter-argument, however, I find myself at somewhat of a loss as to what his material points of disagreement actually are.

---

https://c4ss.org/content/40606

After summarizing my arguments — I repeat, quite fairly — Derek goes on to state, briefly, his reasons for believing that markets will lead to capitalism. But he states these reasons for all intents and purposes as bare assertions, simply restating the positions I attempted to refute without actually providing any new material on why my arguments to the contrary are wrong. Next, in the interest of fairness, he summarizes my arguments regarding countervailing tendencies that would prevent markets from leading to a concentration of capital and restoration of capitalism without the involvement of a state. Then he restates his own original assertions. At no point does he evaluate our respective positions, where they directly contradict each other, in terms of evidence.

Derek's general position is that "[m]arkets tend, in largely spontaneous ways, to generate capitalism ... [I]f we replaced corporate control with market competition, we would, in a relatively short time, be back to concentrated markets." In addition, he feels that markets as such are "to a large extent oppressive and ecologically destructive."

He cites Marx's argument that capital tends to become concentrated, and "competition tends to lead to the removal of smaller enterprises and a drive to monopoly." This happens because "economies of scale mean larger firms often drive out smaller." He acknowledges that I "challenge" Marx's position in "an interesting way" — but provides no material basis for deciding between Marx's position and mine where they differ.

Derek also repeats the standard Marxist arguments regarding capital accumulation and the substitution of physical capital for human labor-power. The consequences are that the first firms to invest in new technology drive out those that don't, and increased capital accumulation leads to increased average firm size and market concentration. He also mentions Brewer's argument, in *Marxist Theories of Imperialism*, that competition, with attendant pressure to cut costs by adopting technical improvements, is "the primary driving force in capitalism." Brewer gives his stamp of approval to the idea that "large-scale production is more efficient than small-scale," and that large firms will be "better able to survive ... in slumps."

All these assertions — and I repeat, unsupported assertions is what they are — either reflect dated technological assumptions that were more appropriate for the early and mid-20th century (if even then), or were never entirely true. Behind all of them is the implicit assumption that efficiency in production directly correlates with capital-intensiveness, scale and cost in production technology. I have argued at length elsewhere[1] that this was only true — if it ever was — during a particular phase of industrial history (and even then, the superior efficiency was to a large extent illusory and resulted from state actions to externalize inefficiency cost or insulate large firms from competition). Although acknowledging I have made such arguments, Derek provides no reason either as to why he finds them unconvincing or why the reader should.

As to the allegedly relentless competitive pressure to cut costs, that's certainly the conventional wisdom. And it's the party line among corporate management, who justify downsizings, speedups and stagnant wages by reference to

[1]Kevin Carson, *The Homebrew Industrial Revolution: A Low-Overhead Manifesto* (2010). See also Carson, "Introduction to the C4SS Edition of Fields, Factories and Workshops Tomorrow" (2014).

the "competitive global economy." But in fact corporate capitalism is characterized far more by the suppression of competition. Competition is mainly for the small players. Far from constantly adopting more efficient technical innovations under the pressure of competition, the large corporations in any particular industry are more likely to collude in spooning out technical improvements in dribs and drabs as they retire old equipment. For example, consider the Big Three US auto companies which, according to the Nader Group, agreed in the early '60s not to introduce various new features until all three companies were ready to introduce them at the same time. Or the major telecommunications companies, which generally provide the same lousy bandwidth and data caps and high rates in any given geographical area, while pocketing the billions in excess rates they collected based on the original promise to build out fiber optic infrastructure.

And throughout industrial history, the major corporate players' relationship to new technology has been characterized by collusion more than competition. Rather than one firm adopting an innovation and taking over an industry, firms have established cartels through the exchange and pooling of patents.

Far from being better able to endure the ups and downs of market competition because they're larger and more efficient, the big players depend on the state to stabilize the marketplace and erect entry barriers to protect them against competition from more efficient small players.

As John Kenneth Galbraith pointed out in *The New Industrial State*, in the very heyday of mass-production capitalism — a system he enthusiastically endorsed — competition is the one thing that large-scale industry cannot deal with. If anything, capital-intensiveness results in fragility, not resilience; the long-term planning horizons of the large manufacturing corporation mean that it has to undertake production with a reasonable assurance that what is produced after several years of design, planning and retooling will be consumed. What large-scale, capital-intensive, mass-production industry needs, above all else, is stability and predictability. Rather than having a superior ability to weather the storms of market competition, large-scale industry is a hothouse flower that depends on the state to reshape the surrounding society to remove as much uncertainty and instability as possible.

That was the primary reason for what Gabriel Kolko, in *The Triumph of Conservatism*, called the "political capitalism" of the Progressive Era regulatory state: state intervention in the market to rationalize the economy and restrict competition to acceptable levels, and enable corporations to extract reasonable, predictable profits in the long run.

Capital-intensiveness carries with it high overhead — and overhead is the essence of fragility. It is the high overhead of large, capital-intensive firms that requires them to have a guaranteed outlet for their product, and creates the imperative of suppressing competition. The higher the overhead, the larger the minimum regular revenue stream required to service it — just to run in place, in other words. The lower the overhead, on the other hand, the more agile and resilient a firm is; likewise the better able it is to ride out bad times without going in the hole, and the more of the revenue stream is income free and clear in good times.

And an increasing share of production technology even within the centralized corporate economy is small-scale, better suited to lean on-demand production for local industrial districts than to a mass consumer society. It's just that the technologies of the new economy are enclosed within corporate walls through the use of state-enforced monopolies — like patents and trademarks — to suppress competition.

Derek also argues that markets "tend to encroach on more and more of human life ... Money tends to move into new areas of society," and ever growing areas of life are incorporated into the cash nexus.

But as David Graeber argued in *Debt*, market exchange (not the predominance of the cash nexus as the primary way of organizing life) has existed on a stable basis in various times and places without turning into capitalism. The exchange of goods with money prices has been a part of economic life in many societies over the past few thousand years. But the hegemony of the cash nexus, and monetization of most of life, to the exclusion of other forms of organizing production and consumption within the social economy is a pathological phenomenon associated with militaristic, aggressive states (as in the Axial age of empires dating from the mid-1st millennium B.C. to the mid-1st millennium A.D., and the even more virulent imperial states that arose in early modern Western Europe and conquered and enslaved most of the world).

And as Derek acknowledges, my enthusiasm for ideas of Ostrom's like natural resource commons (as well as my equal enthusiasm for organizing a growing share of activity through the post-money, abundance-based communism of P2P networks) should make it plain that my idea of a market society is simply one in which market exchange is part of the mix — and not necessarily even a very large part of it.

He also raises the possibilities suggested by Marx himself — for example, he hints that the developing world outside Europe might in some way leapfrog the Western European model of industrial capitalism and evolve directly into communism through such pre-capitalist institutions as the Russian Mir. I think had he lived to see speculations like those of Kropotkin's on the decentralizing potential of electrically powered machinery, in *Fields, Factories and Workshops*,[2] he might have moderated his views on the association between progress and capital-intensiveness and further developed his thoughts on the possibility of much of the world using small-scale, ephemeral technology to bypass the Dark Satanic Mills and go directly towards distributed socialism.

I'm not entirely sure whether Derek has fully taken into account the extent to which my socialistic idea of a "free market society" differs from conventional anarcho-capitalist visions of a society dominated by money exchange and business firms. But that difference leaves a lot of room for agreement between me and Derek on what kind of free society could exist on a stable basis without degenerating into capitalism — perhaps more than Derek has considered. But Derek himself recognizes that there is a great deal of commonality in the kind of post-corporate world we desire, with both of us desiring "a diverse economy, which moves beyond the state and the market to the commons."

> While he sees value in markets, he does to some extent over leap the conventional assumptions, like both Marx and Ostrom, recognising that economic activity extends beyond markets and states. This

[2]http://c4ss.org/wp-content/uploads/2014/08/FactoriesPDF.pdf

> position is vitally important because there is a large and increasingly militant rebellion against corporate neoliberalism taking place. In Europe, parties like Podemos and Syriza have risen on opposition to austerity and corporate control. I am still amazed that my friend Jeremy Corbyn, a lonely left wing MP who was more popular with Greens than his own party, has won a landslide victory to lead the opposition Labour Party here in the UK. In Rojava and the rest of Kurdistan, the revolutionary Kurds, learning from their own participatory experiments and the writings of green anarchist Murray Bookchin, are creating a left libertarian non state.

Like Derek, I have felt enthusiasm not only for Ostrom's thought, but for the rise of offshoot political movements from M15 and Syntagma. I see a great deal of promise in Corbyn's distinction between *state* and *social* ownership — perhaps even some hope of a partial move back towards Colin Ward's vision of public services organized around mutuals and friendly societies instead of government and corporate bureaucracies.

Derek finally notes that to the extent we hope to prevent a "diverse market plus commons economy" from degenerating back into capitalism,

> will require precise mechanism, perhaps some kind of jubilee as advocated in the Torah for wiping out debt and redistributing resources.... While we cannot at a stroke move beyond both markets and states, we can I believe to some extent roll both markets and states back, democratize the economy and create institutional governance which is participatory rather than elitist.

There's much we can agree on here. Like Graeber, I sympathize strongly with the traditional revolutionary program throughout history of abolishing debts and redividing the land. I view the vast majority of today's land titles as artificial and based on past robbery or enclosure, and believe that a libertarian system of ownership (including common ownership) based on appropriation by use and with reasonable standards for constructive abandonment would lead to a state of affairs in which most land was owned by people personally occupying and using it. I believe, likewise, that the vast majority of existing debt is odious and should be wiped clean, and that enforcement of even legitimate debt should be mainly through reputational mechanisms rather than legal enforcement of payment.

In a society based on these principles, and a money system based on the constant mutual advance of credit of the sort Graeber described in the credit-clearing systems of medieval villages, I believe the countervailing measures against the concentration of land and capital would be quite similar to those of the biblical Jubilee system. And in a society where one's right to an aliquot share of natural resource commons was guaranteed by custom, and a major share of one's own subsistence needs could be met within the household economy without permission from (or the payment of rent to) anybody else, the floor of guaranteed comfortable subsistence even in bad times would be quite high by historic standards.

And I repeat, the world in which these things existed (whether that of the Israelite league of the central Palestinian highlands in the Book of Judges or that of the commmoners described by J.M. Neeson) was destroyed primarily by the action of the state.

So to a large extent, I think that once we get beyond the respective connotations that we attach to the word "market" and get to concrete particulars, the potential area of agreement between Derek and me is very large indeed.

CHAPTER

FIVE

COMBATING VULGAR LIBERTARIANISM

KEVIN CARSON

As with Derek Wall, I'm gratified by the thoughtful tone of Steven Horwitz's response to my lead essay.

Where he agrees with me, he makes some good points of his own that add to what I was trying to say — particularly in regard to "free markets" not meaning the domination of society by the cash nexus.

I'm especially pleased to learn of our shared respect for the Ostroms, which he mentions in this regard. The distinction he makes between *governance* and *government*, in discussing Lin Ostrom's work on the commons, is a good one; and his point about "community-based institutional solutions in a free society, particularly on a local scale," is also important. In recognizing (with reference to Vincent

https://c4ss.org/content/40638

Ostrom) that "democracy" need not mean mere majoritarianism, "but instead refers to the participatory way that each of us negotiates with each other to develop rules of social conduct," Steven perceives something that too many mainstream libertarians fail to grasp. "Each time people avoid or resolve conflicts by working with others to solve the problem at hand, they are engaged in the task of democracy."

> The Ostroms shared the concern that community-based solutions to commons problems and our ability to avoid and resolve small-scale conflicts were being crowded out by both the state and the market (in Carson's sense of the "cash nexus"). These other forms of human cooperation were being crushed from both sides by the regulatory state and narrow conceptions of economic institutions. One way of reading this opening point from Carson is that a truly free society opens up that middle ground to a range of Ostrom-style organizational forms. A free market need not be only markets. And an anarchist society is not without governance. The institutional forms that emerge may look much more like the ones we associate with civil society, and Carson rightly notes they are likely to play a much bigger role in a free society.

Exactly!

Where we do disagree on how a society with a freed market would differ from the existing one, a considerable part of the disagreement is a matter of degree, not direction. Steven accuses me of "overstating ... the distortions created by the state" and, while acknowledging that a freed market would differ in many ways from the existing economy, goes on to say that "[w]hat I am much more skeptical about is the *degree* of those differences."

In this regard I can only say that, in my own research on the effects of various general categories of state intervention — perhaps most important among them the large-scale expropriation of land from the peasantries of industrializing Western countries (as well as both land and natural resources from the colonized countries of the Global South), and so-called "intellectual property") — I found it hard to mentally encompass the sheer magnitude of the effect of each one of these categories of intervention taken severally, let alone their cumulative effect. I think a world in which the land of the open fields and the common pasture and waste of Europe, and the land expropriated by the haciendas, Warren Hastings and British East African colonial authorities of the world had all remained in the hands of the original cultivators, would be unrecognizable; certainly the scale of the wage labor market, and the terms on which wage labor was accepted by wage labor, would be far different. A world without the cartelizing effects of patents, and without the service that patents and trademarks currently provide to global corporate control of offshored production, would also be far different. Trying to imagine the cumulative effect of removing these, and other, interventions is — for me at least — still more mind-blowing.

Still, there is a significant amount of disagreement even over the direction of the changes that would result from the removal of state intervention in the economy. Steven finds me guilty of a fault that, in his opinion, I share with much left-libertarian writing: "too many assertions without careful economic argument about what a truly free market would look like ... " Although he concedes that a world without subsidies and other government action to promote centralized long-distance transportation systems might have resulted in "more regional and local" economies, he reminds left-libertarians that "you can't prove a counter-factual."

This is a bit odd coming from an adherent of Austrian economics, which I believe Steven is. Although I am not a follower of that school, I do agree with its tenet that we can often predict *a priori* the *general direction* of the effect that, all other things being equal, a given change will produce.

In the specific case of transportation, he raises the possibility — which he expresses some surprise that I dismissed so quickly — "that ensuring the existence of such transportation systems to facilitate a nationwide market might not be worth it for the private sector." Although Walmart benefits from infrastructure subsidies, "[i]t is not as obvious as Carson seems to think it is that the private sector would not replicate something close to what we have now."

In weighing the question of whether Walmart would find it "worth it" to fund an infrastructure system on the present scale fully at their own cost, all I can say is that cases where people use just as much of something when they have to pay the full cost themselves as they do when using it on somebody else's nickel are pretty rare. A subsidy to any factor input — like transportation — is a subsidy to those firms whose business models rely most heavily on that particular input. So unless large-scale mass-production for large market areas was already more efficient than small-scale production for local markets, we would expect subsidized long-distance transportation to shift the competitive balance to some degree from the latter towards the former. And in fact the supply-push distribution model associated with mass production for large markets carries a considerable number of diseconomies and irrationalities that offset even a portion of the benefit resulting from the transportation subsidies. Far from enabling an increase in overall efficiency, subsidies to long-distance transportation promote a net increase in inefficiency.

Steven also finds fault with my arguments on the superior efficiency of local craft production over mass production for integrating electrical power into manufacturing, and on the industrial district as the ideal model for taking full advantage of such technology.

> I can see no meaningful argument or evidence to support this assertion. It might be true, but there's no reason to think so that I can see. It strikes me as a bit of wishful thinking whereby Carson is able to draw a much greater contrast between the capitalist status quo and his idealized free society.

My lack of citation to back up this claim in the lead essay is a legitimate weakness that Steven has rightly pointed out. It's a claim I've substantiated elsewhere at considerable length and with accompanying documentation (most notably in the first chapter of my book *The Homebrew Industrial Revolution*[1]) that I should have footnoted here as well.

Steven takes issue, finally, with my point about low-cost and ephemeral production technology blurring the lines between "employment" and "unemployment," and between being "in business" and "out of business" (which Marxists

[1]Kevin Carson, *The Homebrew Industrial Revolution: A Low-Overhead Manifesto* (2010), Chapter One.

and much of the mainstream Left make so much of in their prediction that even a non-capitalist market would eventually lead to the reconstitution of capitalism through the cumulative effect of "winners" and "losers" in the competitive marketplace).

> At the end, he argues that in a truly free market we would see less of the sort of unemployment and "going out of business" that we see today thanks to the fluidity of a market with lower capital requirements for entry in smaller-scale production. What Carson appears to misunderstand here is the nature of capital goods, at least in the eyes of the Austrian economists. Even where the scale of production is smaller, "capital" in the abstract does not exist, in contrast to the implication Carson leaves by referring to "capital requirements." Capital comes in the form of specific goods with a limited number of productive uses, not all of which deliver the same value. The same is true of human capital.
>
> The fact that it takes less investment to start a business in a smaller-scale economy doesn't help much when even the smaller-scale machinery that a firm uses cannot be costlessly refit to new uses when demands change or competition favors other firms. The same is true of people. They cannot costlessly "refit" their human capital in the face of exogenous change. Even if production is at smaller scale, inevitable economic change will require costly and time-consuming adjustments by capital and labor, leaving some capital idle and some labor unemployed for some period of time. Perhaps those time periods will be smaller, but again absent more argument,

> that would be mere assertion. But thinking the length of idleness would approach zero is precisely the sort of utopianism of which left-libertarianism is too often guilty.

In this case, I may have left implicit things I should have made explicit in my argument. Although I referred to craft labor quickly shifting back and forth between production runs of different goods, I think I unjustifiably left out a step in my reasoning, and assumed the reader's prior knowledge that craft production is amenable to such rapid shifts without major outlays for physical capital or retraining. Unlike mass production, which uses highly specialized dies and requires extensive retooling to shift between product lines, craft production relies on general purpose machinery that can quickly be reset to produce a wide variety of different products (something also true to a certain extent even within mass-production, as exemplified by the Single Minute Exchange of Dies (SMED) under the Toyota production system). Likewise, craft production in small shops relies on skilled artisans who can adapt their general-purpose machinery to a variety of products without retraining. These, also, are topics I dealt with extensively in my earlier work on the history of production technology, and shouldn't have assumed general readers' familiarity with.

Steven concludes:

> It's my own belief that the underlying economic processes matter more for the relevant costs and benefits than do the distorting effects of the state, and along more margins, than the left-libertarians believe. I might well be wrong, but the danger for

> the left-libertarians is that they are making the same sort of utopian (in the bad sense) promises that have been made by the traditional left. If people are skeptical of that utopianism, it may also backfire onto more mainstream libertarians.
>
> Kevin Carson's essay reminds us not to succumb to what some have called "vulgar libertarianism" in taking the status quo as evidence for what a free society would look like. At the same time, though, that reminder can turn into an equally unproductive utopianism that makes promises that have little evidence to support them and are therefore unlikely to be kept.

I'm gratified — to repeat myself — by Steven's regard for the value of my work in combating vulgar libertarianism. As for my utopian promises with their lack of evidence, I hope my rejoinder will go some way towards remedying that lack.

AUTHORS

1. **Cory Massimino**: Cory Massimino is a fellow at the Center for a Stateless Society, a Students For Liberty Senior Campus Coordinator, and a Young Voices Advocate. His writings have appeared in such publications as *Town Hall*, *Counterpunch*, *The Daily Caller*, *The American Conservative*, *Antiwar.com*, and *The Guardian.* Cory also studies philosophy in central Florida and contributes to the Students For Liberty blog and The Circle Molinari, a student-run left libertarian blog. When he's not eating pizza, he's working to spread the freedom philosophy one slice at a time.

2. **Roy A. Childs**: Roy Alan Childs, Jr. (January 4, 1949 – May 22, 1992) was an American libertarian essayist and critic.
https://en.wikipedia.org/wiki/Roy_Childs

3. **Kevin Carson**: Kevin Carson is a senior fellow of the Center for a Stateless Society (c4ss.org) and holds the Center's Karl Hess Chair in Social Theory. He is a mutualist and individualist anarchist whose written work includes *Studies in Mutualist Political Economy*, *Organization Theory: A Libertarian Perspective*, and

The Homebrew Industrial Revolution: A Low-Overhead Manifesto, all of which are freely available online. Carson has also written for such print publications as *The Freeman: Ideas on Liberty* and a variety of internet-based journals and blogs, including *Just Things*, *The Art of the Possible*, the P2P Foundation, and his own Mutualist Blog.

4. **Roderick T. Long**: Roderick T. Long (A.B. Harvard, 1985; Ph.D. Cornell, 1992) is professor of philosophy at Auburn University, president of the *Molinari Institute* and *Molinari Society*, editor of *The Industrial Radical* and *Molinari Review*, and co-editor of *The Journal of Ayn Rand Studies*. A founding member of the Alliance of the Libertarian Left and senior fellow at the Center for a Stateless Society, Long blogs at *Austro-Athenian Empire* and *Bleeding Heart Libertarians*.

5. **Derek Wall**: Derek Wall is International Coordinator of the Green Party of England and Wales. He writes for the *Morning Star*. His recent books include *The Sustainable Economics of Elinor Ostrom* and *Economics after Capitalism*.

6. **Steve Horwitz**: Steven Horwitz is Charles A. Dana Professor of Economics at St. Lawrence University in Canton, NY, an Affiliated Senior Scholar at the Mercatus Center in Arlington, VA, and a Senior Fellow at the Fraser Institute of Canada. He is the author of three books, including *Hayek's Modern Family: Classical Liberalism and the Evolution of Social Institutions*. He has written extensively on Hayek and Austrian eco-

nomics, monetary theory and history, and American economic history, and he blogs at *Bleeding Heart Libertarians* and *Coordination Problem.* His PhD is from George Mason University and he is a graduate of The University of Michigan.

THE KARL HESS CHAIR IN SOCIAL THEORY

http://c4ss.org/content/10370

The *Karl Hess Scholar in Social Theory* is named in honor of the distinguished anarchist activist and strategist Karl Hess. Hess modeled the radicalism, human decency, commitment to civility, and bridge-building seriousness that the Center for a Stateless Society embraces.

Appointment to the Karl Hess Scholar signals a scholar's capacity to contribute, in outstanding ways, to that interdisciplinary field of social theory – drawing on resources in economics, philosophy, sociology, history, and other fields – known as left-libertarian market anarchism.

C4SS's
MISSION STATEMENT

The Center for a Stateless Society (C4SS) is an anarchist think-tank and media center. Its mission is to explain and defend the idea of vibrant social cooperation without aggression, oppression, or centralized authority.

In particular, it seeks to enlarge public understanding and transform public perceptions of anarchism, while reshaping academic and movement debate, through the production and distribution of market anarchist media content, both scholarly and popular, the organization of events, and the development of networks and communities, and to serve, along with the Alliance of the Libertarian Left and the Molinari Institute, as an institutional home for left market anarchists.

MOLINARI INSTITUTE

MISSION STATEMENT

The form of social organization known as the State, an increasingly virulent parasite on civil society, is entering the final stages of an unsustainable growth that threatens the existence of civilisation itself.

The mission of the Molinari Institute is to promote understanding of the philosophy of Market Anarchism as a sane, consensual alternative to the hypertrophic violence of the State.

The Institute takes its name from Gustave de Molinari (1819-1912), originator of the theory of Market Anarchism.

The Molinari Institute is a 501(c)(3) tax-exempt organisation.

ALLIANCE
OF THE
LIBERTARIAN LEFT
PREAMBLE

The Alliance of the Libertarian Left is a multi-tendency coalition of mutualists, agorists, voluntaryists, geolibertarians, left-Rothbardians, green libertarians, dialectical anarchists, radical minarchists, and others on the libertarian left, united by an opposition to statism and militarism, to cultural intolerance (including sexism, racism, and homophobia), and to the prevailing corporatist capitalism falsely called a free market; as well as by an emphasis on education, direct action, and building alternative institutions, rather than on electoral politics, as our chief strategy for achieving liberation.

C4SS's
EDITORIAL POLICY

The Center for a Stateless Society (C4SS) commissions and distributes media content designed to challenge the state: To undermine the false perception of its legitimacy, demonstrate its irrelevance to truly solving social and economic problems, and encourage its abolition. At no time will any C4SS publication implicitly or explicitly support the state's continuation or augmentation.

C4SS's publications will convey a positive vision of voluntary, peaceful cooperation as the basis for flourishing life in society; they will seek to foster not only the free exchange of goods and services but also the many other kinds of voluntary interaction that help to make social existence viable and attractive. Thus, they will urge the abolition of all those privileges that impede peaceful cooperation, while unequivocally rejecting the privilege-riddled capitalism so frequently mistaken for a genuinely freed market. And they will help to realize a culture free from authoritarianism, exclusion, submission, and deprivation — whether effected and sustained violently or non-violently — as well as aggressive violence.

C4SS emphasizes education, direct action, and the construction of alternative institutions, rather than electoral politics, as strategies for achieving liberation.

While its basic commitments will be consistently embodied in C4SS's publications, not every C4SS author will embrace all of them, and the C4SS's core values are reflected in part in its willingness to publish the work of a broad range of thinkers who oppose the state and who value economic and cultural freedom.

SOURCES

Morton S. Baratz. "Corporate Giants and the Power Structure," in Richard Gillam, ed., *Power in Postwar America* (Boston: Little, Brown, and Co., 1971).

Harry C. Boyte. *The Backyard Revolution: Understanding the New Citizen Movement* (Philadelphia: Temple University Press, 1980).

Don Carney. "Dwayne's World," at http://www.motherjones.com/mother_jones/JA95/carney.html

Alfonso Chardy. "Reagan Aides and the 'Secret' Government" *Miami Herald* 5 July 1987, at http://www.totse.com/en/conspiracy/the_new_world_order/scrtgovt.html

Noam Chomsky. *Class Warfare: Interviews with David Barsamian.* (Monroe, Maine: Common Courage Press, 1996).

Chomsky. "How Free is the Free Market?" *Resurgence* no. 173. http://www.oneworld.org/second_opinion/chomsky.html

Chomsky. *World Orders Old and New* (New York: Columbia University Press, 1998).

Citizens for Tax Justice. "GOP Leaders Distill Essence of Tax Plan: Surprise! It's Corporate Welfare" 14 September 1999, at http://www.ctj.org/pdf/corp0999.pdf

Alexander Cockburn. "The Jackboot State: The War Came Home and We're Losing It" *Counterpunch* 10 May 2000, at http://www.counterpunch.org/jackboot.html

Maurice Dobbs. *Studies in the Development of Capitalism* (London: Routledge and Kegan Paul, Ltd, 1963).

Gary Elkin. *Benjamin Tucker—Anarchist or Capitalist?* at http://flag.blackened.net/davo/anarchism/tucker/an_or_cap.html

Elkin. *Mutual Banking*. Available through http://www.subsitu.com

Friedrich Engels. "Anti-Duhring." *Marx and Engels, Collected Works* v. 25 (New York: International Publishers, 1987).

Edgar Friedenberg. *The Disposal of Liberty and Other Industrial Wastes* (Garden City, N.Y.: Anchor, 1976).

Robert Goldstein.*Political Repression in America: 1870 to the Present* (Cambridge, New York: Schenkman Publishing Co', 1978).

David M. Gordon. *Fat and Mean: The Corporate Squeeze of Working Americans and the Myth of Management Downsizing* (New York: The Free Press, 1996).

William B. Greene. *Mutual Banking* (New York: Gordon Press, 1849, 1974).

Benjamin Grove. "Gibbons Backs Drug Monopoly Bill," *Las Vegas Sun* 18 February 2000, at http://www.ahc.umn.edu/NewsAlert/Feb00/022100NewsAlert/44500.htm

J.L. and Barbara Hammond. *The Town Labourer* (1760-1832) 2 vols. (London: Longmans, Green & Co., 1917).

Hammonds. *The Village Labourer* (1760-1832) (London: Longmans, Green & Co., 1913). Michael Harrington. *Socialism* (New York: Bantam, 1970, 1972).

Harrington. *The Twilight of Capitalism* (Simon and Schuster, 1976).

Hearings on Global and Innovation-Based Competition. FTC, 29 November 1995, at http://www.ftc.gov/opp/gc112195.pdf

John Judis. "Bare Minimum: Goodies for the Rich Hidden in Wage Bill," *The New Republic* 28 October 1996, in *Project Censored Yearbook 1997* (New York: Seven Stories Press, 1997).

Frank Kofsky. *Harry S. Truman and the War Scare of 1948* (New York: St. Martin's Press, 1993).

Peter Kropotkin. *Mutual Aid: A Factor of Evolution* (New York: Doubleday, Page & Co., 1909).

William Lazonick. *Business Organization and the Myth of the Market Economy* (Cambridge University Press, 1991).

Lazonick. *Competitive Advantage on the Shop Floor* (Cambridge and London: Harvard University Press, 1990).

Chris Lewis. "Public Assets, Private Profits," *Multinational Monitor*, in *Project Censored Yearbook 1994* (New York: Seven Stories Press, 1994).

Tiber Machan. "On Airports and Individual Rights," *The Freeman: Ideas on Liberty.* February 1999.

Steven A. Marglin. "What Do Bosses Do? The Origins and Functions of Hierarchy in Capitalist Production–Part I" *Review of Radical Political Economics* 6:2 (Summer 1974).

Karl Marx and Friedrich Engels. *Capital* vol. 1, *Collected Works* v. 35 (New York: International Publishers, 1996).

Seymour Melman. *Profits Without Production.* (New York: Alfred A. Knopf, 1983).

C. Wright Mills. *The Power Elite* (Oxford University Press, 1956, 2000).

David Montgomery. *The Fall of the House of Labor* (New York: Cambridge University Press,

1979).

Montgomery. *Workers Control in America* (New York: Cambridge University Press, 1979).

Richard K. Moore. "Escaping the Matrix" *Whole Earth* (Summer 2000).

Frank Morales. "U.S. Military Civil Disturbance Planning: The War at Home" *Covert Action Quarterly* 69, Spring-Summer 2000, at http://infowar.net/warathome/warathome.html

David F. Noble. *America By Design: Science, Technology, and the Rise of Corporate Capitalism* (New York: Alfred A. Knopf, 1977).

Noble. *Forces of Production: A Social History of Industrial Automation* (New York: Alfred A. Knopf, 1984).

Martin Khor Kok Peng. *The Uruguay Round and Third World Sovereignty* (Penang, Malaysia: Third World Network, 1990).

Chakravarthi Raghavan. *Recolonization: GATT, the Uruguay Round & the Third World* (Penang, Malaysia: Third World Network, 1990).

J. B. Robertson. *The Economics of Liberty.* (Mineapolis: Herman Kuehn, 1916).

Paul Rosenberg. "The Empire Strikes Back: Police Repression of Protest From Seattle to L.A." *L.A. Independent Media Center* 13 August 2000, at http://www.r2kphilly.org/pdf/empire-strikes.pdf

Murray Rothbard. "Confessions of a Right-Wing Liberal," in Henry J. Silverman, ed., *American Radical Thought* (Lexington, Mass.: D.C. Heath and Co., 1970).

Rothbard. *Man, Economy, and State: A Treatise on Economic Principles* (Los Angeles: Nash Publishing, 1952, 1970).

Rothbard. *Power and Market* (New York: New York University Press, 1977).

Adam Smith. *The Wealth of Nations.* Great Books edition (Encyclopedia Brittanica, Inc., 1952).

Testimony of Chairman Alan Greenspan. *U. S. Senate Committee on Banking, Housing, and Urban Affairs.* 26 February 1997, at http://www.federalreserve.gov//boarddocs/hh/1997/february/testimony/htm

E. P. Thompson. *The Making of the English Working Class* (New York: Vintage, 1963, 1966).

Benjamin Tucker. *Instead of a Book, by a Man Too Busy to Write One* (New York: Haskell House Publishers, 1897 1969).

Immanuel Wallerstein. *Historical Capitalism* (London, New York: Verso, 1983).

Diane Cecilia Weber. "Warrior Cops: The Ominous Growth of Paramilitarism in American Police Departments" *Cato Briefing Paper* No.

50, 26 August 1999, at http://www.cato.org/pubs/briefs/bp-050es.html

Mark Zepezauer and Arthur Naiman. *Take the Rich Off Welfare* (Odonian Press/Common Courage Press, 1996).

The Fly & The Ant

The ant and the fly were bitterly arguing about who was more important. The fly presented her case first. "Do you really mean to compare yourself to my exalted status? I pass my time among the altars, I wander through the temples of the gods; whenever there is a sacrifice, I am the first to taste all the entrails; I can sit on the head of the king if I want and I enjoy the forbidden kisses of all the married women; I do not work and yet I reap the very best of all the spoils. What has life given you that can compare with all that I have, you country bumpkin!" The ant replied, "It is truly a wonderful thing to dine at the gods' table, but only for someone whom the gods have invited, not for someone whom they hate. You say that you frequent their altars? Agreed, but you are driven away as soon as you arrive. As for the kings you mention and the women's kisses, you are boasting about something that it is shameful to mention. Moreover, if you do no work then it is no surprise that you have nothing at hand when you need it. I, on the other hand, assiduously gather a store of grain for the winter, while I see you feeding on manure piled up against the walls. Later on, when the cold winds make you shrivel up and die, I am safe and at peace in my well-furnished abode. Now that it is summer you try to provoke me, but in winter you have nothing to say. That should be enough to take the edge off your pride."

This sort of fable shows how to recognize those people who extol themselves for empty deeds and those whose noble qualities are marked by solid accomplishments.

Translation by Laura Gibbs, from *Æsop's Fables* (Oxford: Oxford University Press, 2002).

Donate Today!

The Center for a Stateless Society (C4SS) functions on the enthusiasm of writers and volunteers, but it is the continued donations of supporters that keeps us going and growing. We have big plans and even bigger dreams for C4SS and we need your help.

Fundraising is not begging or charity. It is a barometer of success, support and professionalism. It is about offering an opportunity to participate in the project, the task at hand. So we ask you, dear supporters, let us know how we are doing and play a crucial part in our success by giving to C4SS.

C4SS's parent institution, the Molinari Institute, is a tax-exempt 501(c)(3) nonprofit organization; hence donations to the Molinari Institute – and thus to the Center for a Stateless Society – are tax-deductible. The Molinari Institute's tax identification number is 20-3731375.

www.ingramcontent.com/pod-product-compliance
Lightning Source LLC
Chambersburg PA
CBHW060238290526
45789CB00001B/100

* 9 7 8 1 5 3 9 4 8 8 7 3 6 *